CHEYENNE (

I PRAY JESUS
SPEAKS TO YOU —

ENJOY.

ABOVE

BRYAN LINDGREN

ALL ELSE

THANK YOUS: MY WIFE KAYLA RAE FOR SUPPORTING ME TO WRITE A BOOK THAT MATTERED AND WAS HONEST. I LOVE YOU. CHRIS SEIDEL FOR READING MY RAMBLING THOUGHTS AND HELPING ME PUT TOGETHER SOMETHING PEOPLE MIGHT ACTUALLY BE INTERESTED IN READING. DOUG HARKNESS FOR NOT SLEEPING AND MAKING THIS BOOK HAPPEN. STEVE DECOY FOR INVESTING IN ME AND EDITING MY MANUSCRIPT. THANK YOU TO ANYBODY WHO READ THROUGH THIS BOOK AND GAVE ME FEEDBACK. THANK YOU TO MY CHURCH NEWLIFE.TV FOR BEING THE KIND OF PLACE WHERE JESUS WINS. YOU KNEW ME AT EVERY STAGE OF THIS BOOK AND I AM GRATEFUL FOR THAT.

"BEHIND EVERY BEAUTIFUL THING THERE
HAS BEEN SOME KIND OF PAIN."
- BOB DYLAN

"MY GRACE IS SUFFICIENT FOR YOU, FOR
POWER IS PERFECTED IN WEAKNESS."
- 2 CORINTHIANS 12:9

ALL OF THIS IS TRUE. 100%. IT REALLY HAPPENED. SOME OF THE NAMES HAVE BEEN CHANGED AND OTHERS HAVEN'T. SOME OF THE NAMES I CHANGED AND THEN CHANGED BACK TO THE REAL NAME BECAUSE I FIGURED WHO REALLY CARES. IT DOESN'T MATTER. WHAT MATTERS IS THAT THIS REALLY HAPPENED.

THAT'S ALL THAT MATTERS.

BAD TIMING
FEBRUARY, *JUNIOR YEAR OF HIGH SCHOOL*

Ever notice how basically everything in life has bad timing? No, bad timing isn't even right--it's more like horrible coincidences that are too perfect to ignore. It's probably some law of something or other in nature--like this obnoxious subatomic principle: *any sucky thing that can happen, most likely will happen*. I get why some cultures assume the gods are pissed off and hurling meteors at us, spewing hurricanes, and tangling our headphones in knots in our backpacks. I get that. If you've ever been in high school, you get that too.

Let me back up.
The best way to start all of this is with Anna.

I felt stuck. Not just stuck, but bored. Life felt like an endless cycle of loops. Like a GIF just playing over and over and over. There was nothing new. Nothing to be excited about. I wasn't hopeless, I just wasn't at that time hopeful.

It's Valentine's Day of my junior year. I'm not like some people who hate Valentine's Day. Whatever, so it's a stupid holiday. I get it's just an excuse for overly-obsessed couples to buy worthless junk for each other and make out; but mostly I'm fine with the whole thing. I have never been the dude carrying a giant stuffed dog and chocolates into school for my boo-thang. I've never even had a girlfriend on Valentine's Day. I'm fine with that too. Most Valentine's Days my mom leaves me a surfing magazine on the kitchen table, along with some chocolate.

Oh *frick,* I'm just realizing how lame it sounds that my mom is the only one giving me anything on Valentine's Day. Okay, *okay,* I can see how you'd think I have no friends, but that's not true. I just have an awesome mom who fully supports me on this national holiday of chalky heart-shaped candy and hickeys. (Can we finally acknowledge that hickeys are the absolute most disgusting thing, just below undie-stains--I'm serious, what the heck is that nonsense? Girls: if any dude is trying to pull that crap and vacuum bruise your neck, he's not worth that kind of attention. I'm serious, if you're wearing turtlenecks because Trevor is basically a neck suction machine; you're better than that, it's gross, leave Trevor.)

Valentine's Day morning I felt fine but by third period I knew I was sick. It was a head cold or something. I went home.

Anna Sofia is the classic girl next door. To be clear, she isn't actually next-door. We live across town from each other. She's an only child; her parents are from Spain and have sharp accents. They're much older than any of my friend's parents, her father has a rich white beard and her mother has an elegant, almost elderly Spanish beauty in the way she carries herself. Her father's English is only slightly better than her mother's. Their house is on the water and feels like the home of well-off professors with evidences of years of travel-- framed pictures, old books on dark toned shelves, masterfully large rugs, tall decorative beer steins with the names of different European cities written in bold typeface.

Anna has a convertible, but not a snobby girl convertible, a Volkswagen Cabriolet convertible that every one of my friends wants to drive, but none of them know how to operate a manual.

Anna doesn't have to try to be trendy or bold. She is simply who she is and is liked for it. In some ways, she is the girl every guy really wants to date in high school. She's a girl comfortable living in the world she's been given.

———

We started talking casually a few weeks before February 14th. Some of her friends were dating a few of my friends. We'd known each other as sort-of friends since eighth grade but never been close.
Once, at a birthday party in ninth grade, we briefly danced to the same song together in a basement, realizing halfway in that we were the only ones dancing and that everybody was *oohing* and *aweing* from the sidelines while the two of us shook our tail feathers to aggressive rap.

If that isn't the definition of love, I don't know what is.

There was for sure chemistry; although she didn't really acknowledge me much after, I knew that we were right for each other.

Too many of us spend too much time-- especially as teenagers--knowing we are right for somebody who doesn't know we are right for them.

Junior year is strange compared to sophomore year. Sophomore year I knew who I was. I had me all figured out. Inside out I had me dialed in. I did okay in school. Not like real good, but good for me. My life felt like it fit together. My friends, we were this tribe of skater, surfer, artists who spray painted the word 'renegade' on our t-shirts and dated popular girls with rich dads. We got part time jobs. We took over the town on long-boards. All the parts of life mostly made sense.

Everybody is all tense and stressed out now. Lots of the couples who were solid last year either broke up or fight all the time or just flat out try and murder each other over social media. School has gotten more difficult all of a sudden. It's like I am holding tight to what was awesome about sophomore year, but it's slipping away. The friends who still have girlfriends have gotten way too serious. They talk about marriage. They basically said 'screw you' to anybody they once knew. Junior year is lonely. There are a million people everywhere but everybody feels alone. Not to mention college looming over all of us.

———

I wake up to the doorbell ringing.

I've been asleep all afternoon on the couch. My throat feels like it's a scratching post for a cat. My nose is running. This week is not my week. Too many assignments, not enough sleep. When I take naps in the middle of the afternoon I usually end up regretting them. Some scientist I'm sure could do some kind of case study on my naps and find all sorts of interesting details about what happens to my body. The closest example I can come to is: I die. I blackout. I am not there.

Everything in me shuts off.
I will close my eyes, expecting to maybe doze off for a few minutes and wake up four hours later forgetting where I am.

It's worse when I am sick. I go into a primal hibernation and wake up not sure if I am awake, or dreaming, or even alive.

I wake up on the living room couch, drool puddled at my chin, sweat soaking my shirt, half my body falling off the couch. I hear the shrill ring of the doorbell and my first thought is *don't answer it*.

It keeps ringing.

Curiosity gets the best of me. I am wondering who's at the door in the middle of the day. My friends just barge in. A neighbor wouldn't wait this long. Somebody knows I am here.

When I wake up from a nap my legs don't work. I throw my weight into each step. I limp past the television, my feet slipping on the hardwood floor.

She's standing at the door in a Levi's jean jacket and red rain boots. My stomach lifts into my throat. There's no air in the room. Anna Sofia sees me. My eyes are dull and feel heavy. Hers flash full of life. They are full of "hello" and "good to see you" when they catch mine.

I need to be clear, I'm wearing sweatpants from a few years ago that are too small. I'm also not wearing a shirt. This is not attractive. Some guys would think this is awesome. I'm not self-conscience about my body. I'm just skinny the way children are skinny--boney with outlined ribs. It's not that I'm embarrassed; it's just not my best foot forward.

I also have that imprint on my side that the fabric from a couch leaves on bare skin. It looks like I have a disease or hives or should see a dermatologist.

The Cabriolet is sitting in my driveway. I open the door and she just sort of shrugs and I don't know what to say. The nerves in my stomach are getting weird with my just waking up and I'm making this face that basically says, 'I'm confused, scared and maybe a little sad'. She hands me this *thing*. As if to help clarify her presence at my doorstep in the middle of the day and as a response to the frightened disorientation plastered all over my face.

I reach out and grab the *thing*. And examine its *thingness*.

"I missed you at school," She says with another shrug.

It's a bunch of Dr. Peppers (my favorite soda) with balloons and a card at the top that says, "Feel Better!"

The nap's side effects, though normal for my nap routine, are preventing me from completely engaging in the conversation or showing what would be considered *normal human behavior*. First, I keep yawning repeatedly, sending a clear message to Anna that I find her incredibly boring. Which I do not. When I yawn, I try and stop, which makes the yawn more aggressive and pronounced. I look like a lion yawning. Have you ever seen a lion yawn? It's confrontational. I've yawned eleven times since I answered the door. She probably thinks I am a very strange creature. Next, I am not wearing socks. I need to wear socks whenever other humans are present. This is not a hard and fast rule for all people but it certainly is for me. My feet are disgusting. Not in a 'I don't really like my feet' way, more like people sometimes vomit in their mouths when they see my feet. They are wide feet, webbed slightly at the toes, hairy with long black patches, and toe nails that, despite my best grooming and sawing and hacking, are grotesquely jagged and hued yellow. I know, I know, I'm basically a monster. Hence, I have to wear socks.

When I was in eighth grade I forgot to keep my shoes on at a beach party. There was an incident between my big toenail and an inflatable inner tube. It all happened so fast. Courtney was on the tube. Courtney was popular. My foot hit the side of the inner tube. For most humans this would have been harmless but for me and my condition, it was a disaster. I can remember hearing the shrill whine of air exiting the hole that my nail had just carved out of the thick rubber. Courtney began to sink and scream and look at me with these evil, over-mascaraed eyes that said, "I will destroy you". Maybe I'm over-exaggerating the story in my mind, all I know is it was traumatic. A bunch of the cute popular girls called me "The Claw" for the rest of the school year and would draw red scratch marks on their arms with pens and yell, "the claw scratched me" in class right in front of me.

I'm so paranoid she'll look down at my feet that I scrunch my toes under my feet, standing upright like a disoriented ballerina. Which you can imagine is only drawing attention to my feet.

Also after I take naps, my eyes water. I don't know why. I'm not talking about a little single tear. I'm talking *slicing onions* kind of tears. I'm talking borderline weeping. I can feel tears--actual *tears* forcefully sliding down my face. I'm balancing on my toes and crying. I'm a mess.

"This is for me?" I ask.
She tells me it is. That it's my favorite soda. *Oh! OH! OH!* And she almost forgot, from her purse she pulls a DVD- *Footloose*.

"It's my favorite movie ever. I watch it every time I'm sick."

I'm frozen. My brain begins to fire fast-paced dialog:

Brain:
This is some sort of trap.

Me:
I don't think so--I think this might be for real.

Brain:
No, don't fall for it. It's too good to be true. She has a knife, or a gun, or explosives, or poison! She poisoned the Dr. Pepper! Rodenticide. Arsenic. Agent Orange. Check her search history, I'll bet you'll find "how to poison unsuspecting, love-struck teenagers" right at the top next to "where to bury the body of hopelessly dumb high-school boys who were too trusting to not see the signs of sudden death."

Me:
Don't say that! You're ruining this for me. Now I'm overthinking it.

Brain:
Or it's a prank. Like a hidden camera show. She's really Ashton Kutcher. She's Ashton Kutcher dressed up like your crush and there are cameras somewhere and Ashton Kutcher will be like "you just got Punk'd! High School Crush Edition!"

Me:
That show is super old. It's not even on TV anymore. Good try.

Brain:
Maybe this is the big comeback episode?
Didn't think of that, did you?
Me:
She's not Ashton Kutcher.

Brain:
You don't know that. Where's your proof?

Me:
That she's not Ashton Kutcher?

Brain:
Yeah.

Me: I guess I don't have any.

Brain:
Listen: guys like you, guys who get surf
magazines from their moms on Valentine's
Day, don't get surprise visits from cute,
emotionally-stable girls with great taste in
classic rock, who have a shot at a decent
college, and smell like vanilla, and have been
to Switzerland, and can rap all the words to
Snoop Dogg songs, and snowboard, and have
pleasant shiny hair, and can roll their r's...
they just don't okay. This just isn't realistic.

Me:
You just won't let me have anything good
without trying to rationalize all of it.

Brain:
That's literally my job.

Me:
Well, you should stop. It's annoying.

Brain:
That's called denial, and I'm trying to protect you from having a mental breakdown. That's my job. Also, protecting you from poison and danger.

Me:
You're going to jinx this whole thing.

Brain:
I'M SAVING YOU!

Me:
YOU ARE RUINING THIS!

Brain:
Remember that time, on that family vacation, when you thought it would be a good idea to stick your entire giant head in the railings on the staircase at your grandma's house because you told your cousin, and I quote, "my head will totally fit in there" and remember what happened? Do you?

Me:
Yes.

Brain:
What happened?

Me:
You told me it made no sense and that I would for sure get stuck.

Brain:
And what happened?

Me:
My head *did* fit, but my ears got stuck when I tried to pull my head out.

Brain:
Right. And your cousin left you there, hunched over and stuck with your head in the railings. Just standing there quietly by yourself while your whole family was in the other room having a wonderful time. We were stuck there until your Uncle Lee meandered by and happened to notice you.

Me:
Okay that was pretty bad.

Brain:
Pretty bad? Do you remember them greasing up the back of your ears? Do you remember

that feeling? Because, that's what my job is, to make sure this stuff doesn't happen.

Me:
I get it but that was like four years ago.

Brain:
THAT WAS LAST YEAR!

Me:
No.

Brain:
Yes, yes, yes--it was last summer. You had just got your license.

Me:
Frick! You're right. That's so embarrassing.

Brain:
My job is to protect you.

Me:
I think this is legit.

Brain:
I'm just saying. I want you to remember Uncle Lee greasing up the back of your ears while your grandpa pushes on the top of your head. I want you to save that image. Because, that's what I don't want to happen to you.

I have the same pale, stupid grin on my boring face, while she's just standing there at the door. I interrupt the silence with something about how I heard Dr. Pepper is made with prunes, and this is why it's good for you. She gives me a smile, hugs me, and says she has to get home.

Then she's gone. Just like that. I'm standing there with my arms wide, bear-hugging balloons, DVDs, and Dr. Pepper and just sort of blankly wondering what was happening in my life.

Brain:
Please, just be careful.

JUNK DRAWER
MARCH, *JUNIOR YEAR OF HIGH SCHOOL*

I am standing in the kitchen. I can hear my mom from across the room. Her voice is barely louder than the voices from the TV. She's talking quickly. Her words are spilling into one another. She sounds nervous. Not the typical prowess she has when we talk.

"I would like you to come with us for spring break," she says, "I think you need to get out of the house."

The last part she says slower. It sounds like a plea. The words just sit there between us instead of floating away like most words do. I stare at them. Analyze their form. They're heavy. Heavier than anything she's said in weeks. The silence between us is puncturing. Shouting. Roaring. Cracking.

I have scissors in my hands.

They are regular kitchen scissors. The kind you keep in a drawer with rubber bands, ballpoint pens, stamps, loose change, plastic parts to things long forgotten, receipts, chargers for a phone you don't have anymore, crayons, strange keys. All the things that don't have a place.

I feel like a thing that should live in this drawer.
I feel like less of a person, and more of a memory of a person who used to be a person. I used to be a person. Now I feel like the charger to a phone long gone.

My insides hurt.

I didn't have a name for this feeling at first. I just knew I felt distant from who I had been simply weeks before. I couldn't quantify it, and I had no control over it. Then once I had a name for it, I didn't want to say it because that would make it too real.

It's the reason we don't talk about our depression. Because, if we can just shove it in a dark corner we think it might just go away. But depression grows in darkness.
Depression starts as a single cell organism, but left unnamed and in the dark, there is multiplication. Mitosis takes one single thought and duplicates it. Left for long enough, the sheer volume of this process spawns an epidemic within us.

The scissors in my hands are the same scissors we've always had. Forever. Seriously, as long as I can remember we've had these exact scissors with the orange handles. I probably used these as a kid to cut out snowmen at Christmas. Isn't it interesting that there are things in our lives that follow us?

I didn't always feel like a member of the junk drawer. I used to feel like a functioning part of society, of my family, and my school. Now, I feel like an actor in my own life that isn't right for the role. I was miscast as Bryan. I can't do a good Bryan. It feels like a bad impression. I'm an imposter. A sloppy impersonator. I can't be Bryan. I don't even know who Bryan is. I want to close myself in that drawer, I want to see the darkness spill over and never wake up. Me and the broken sunglasses, and paper clips, and nail files, and old checkbooks. Locked away forever.

"Bry, did you hear me?"

I look up from the scissors to my mom on the couch. Her head is facing away from me. I don't say anything. Not that I don't want to, but I can't. Physically, I can't. It's been this way since that night. I have words, but they just sit inside me as if it would take a great force of effort to heave them out onto the floor. I'm too drained. Empty. Annoyed.

There is a guy in the Bible--his name is Job. Job has all these horrible things happen to him. His whole world has shattered all around him. He's standing in the mangled pieces of his life. A life he liked. He loved. He looked forward to waking up into. Then the whole thing hits the fan. His life falls apart all around him and he says,

"And now my life seeps away.
 Depression haunts my days.
At night my bones are filled with pain,
 which gnaws at me relentlessly."

Have you ever felt like this? This is how I feel. Like my life is seeping away. I keep thinking about depression haunting my days. At school I feel this cloud of weakness. People, friends, teachers have called me at home on the phone, have pulled me aside in class to whisper, "You don't seem like yourself."

Depression is a leaky faucet.
All of what makes you who you are spilling out slowly.
Drop by drop.

I am way past lying and saying *I'm just fine.*
Most the time I simply respond,

"I am not myself." I look them in the face confessing,
"I have no idea who I am now."

They put their hand on my shoulder, they say they are here for me, they say I've been under a lot of stress with classes. They ask if they can help.
I say, "If you find the real me, I'd like to know, I'd like to shake his hand and get him back into his life. I'm tired of holding his spot."

They stare at me confused. I stare back also confused. We are both confused.

They say they are worried. Concerned. They say they don't know what happened.

But I know what happened. It all happened after Valentine's Day. That was the beginning of the end. My English teacher, Ms. Tucker, told me she was frightened by some of the essays I'd written recently. She said they were pretty dark. To be clear, Ms. Tucker was gone for a whole month because she went crazy. No, for real, somebody came in our fourth period class, somebody from the school administration and straight up told us this would be our new English teacher Mrs. So-and-so, they'd be subbing for a while because Ms. Tucker was working through some *mental health issues*. Ironically, I thought it was funny at the time. I don't think it's funny now. Now, those three words have teeth on them. They bark and bite, roar and ravage, chomp and clench down all over me.

Mental health issues.

If Ms. Tucker says your essays are dark, you might have a problem, *just saying.*
I look down at the floor beneath me. I've been slicing up a women's athletic wear catalog my sister gets in the mail. Cutting the faces of jogging blondes, yoga mats, running shoes, and kick boxers into small triangles onto the floor. Tiny triangles scattered across the hardwood floor in thin piles. I watch them fall slowly.

I think about my mom sitting in the living room trying to help get me out of the house. I wonder if she knows. Not just *thinks-* but really knows. That something inside me is not right. That I am dissolving. That I am worried about what I will do if it gets worse. If I lose any more of me, there won't be anything left.

Have you ever felt like this?
That you are being erased from the inside out?
Have you ever worried that you might hurt yourself?

Maybe you tried to hurt yourself. Maybe you tried in your imagination. Maybe you wished you tried. Maybe you had dreams where you tried. Maybe you smoke weed so you don't try. Or drink. Or play videogames. Or eat too much. Or cry alone. Or take it out on other people. We all have our ways of covering up pain.

Maybe you go to school and feel tormented by your thoughts only to come home to face overwhelming loneliness.
Job goes onto say,

"I cry to you, O God, but you don't answer.
 I stand before you, but you don't even look."

I talk to God and don't get anything on the other end. I know he's getting my texts. I know he's hearing my prayers. At least I think he is.

The scissors in my hands opening and retracting,
The pages falling to the ground like confetti.

I imagine getting in a time machine and traveling to specific times over the last few months and punching myself in the ear.

Saying,

"I'm you from the future!"

Holding myself by the collar of my shirt, my knuckles tight up against my throat, looking myself in my eyes and saying,

"You're messing up everything."

I see myself marching in and interrupting key moments, moments with friends, moments alone, at school, with *her* and grabbing myself and throwing me onto a glass coffee table, the glass shattering into tiny fragments, I kick myself in the spleen. Slap myself in the face. Push myself into the wall. I ask what's wrong with me. I make myself see. I make my stubborn self realize what I'm doing. "You are only hurting yourself!" I yell.

I say, "Why did you have to be so selfish?"

But I'm really just talking to myself. I'm really just asking myself that question. Right there in the kitchen. I don't need a time machine to ask myself why I am so selfish.
Little slivers sailing out as I get closer and closer to the binding with the staples and my own hand. Inch by inch until there isn't anything left.

"And now my life seeps away."

But, I am getting ahead of myself.

MY OWN PERSONAL RENAISSANCE
TEN YEARS AFTER JUNIOR YEAR OF HIGH
SCHOOL

People used to think we were the center of
our galaxy. Then a guy named Kepler came
along and said, *maybe not*. Galileo used his
fancy telescope and said, "yeah the sun is
definitely the center of the galaxy." Thousands
of years of believing one thing and *boom* all of
a sudden that thing isn't true anymore.

The sun was the center. Everything didn't orbit
around us. This was a big deal. It was a big
deal because we weren't the center of the
galaxy.

This discovery came during the Renaissance
Period, a period of history marked by
incredible creativity, exploration, and
discovery. It also marked the end of the Dark
Ages.

There is something that happens in our lives
when we take ourselves out of the center--
when we say everything doesn't revolve
around us--when we put God in the center,
that we begin to sense an incredible

movement of creativity and discovery in our life. We leave the Dark Age of our life and enter a new place.

You might feel like you are in the Dark Ages.

I am twenty-seven years old, and I want you to hear this: you are not the center of the universe. You are a part of the whole thing, you are in beautiful orbit, you matter, but you are not the center.

That's where God sits.
But it can feel like we are always wrestling God for that spot.

There's a story in the Bible where a guy by the name of Jacob wrestles with God. You read that right--he *wrestles* the Creator of the universe. Like physically. And they aren't like horsing around. He picks a fight with God. He's lost, he's depressed, and he's tired of pretending he's okay--he feels like his life has no purpose.

The strangest part of the whole story--the funny, unpredictable, bizarre thing is this guy, Jacob--he wins.

First, a little bit on the Bible and faith.

I believe in the Bible. When I talk about faith, I am not talking about a mindset that isn't curious, or exploring, or questioning, or creative, or is in someway naïve to truth.

Actually, I am convinced of the exact opposite. Faith is endlessly curious, furiously exploring, deeply questioning, and bursting at the seams with creativity.

Somebody once told me they thought faith was boring.

Faith, he said, was a stagnant, oppressive, destructive, and overall mostly a *blahh* way to live. He said it was closed-minded. I get that. I have seen, felt, and heard people who claim to have faith who sound angrier, more hateful and backwards than somebody who claims to have no faith. Some people use their faith like a weapon against others.

Faith to these people can look more like a prison cell than freedom.

I've seen lots of people who say they have faith in the Bible, yet act in this way that basically makes me want to say, 'yeah no thanks, I think I'll be fine without that.' Or they just want to prove they're right, while you just want to shove your head down a garbage disposal.

And still, I say that there is something undeniably good at the bottom of everything. There is something humming, at the quantum level of the universe that's not meaningless, or chaotic, or a black hole of nothing. The universe is expanding, and with it, I see this giant mystery all wrapped up in these things I keep finding in faith and the Bible.

We live in this world where it can seem like it's people who have faith against those who don't. Like you have to pick a side. It's like there is this epic dodgeball game of back-and-forth and on one side you have this group that says they don't have faith and on the other you have people with faith.

Except, everybody has faith.

It's not a question of faith or no faith--we all put faith in something. Whether it's a faith in that *right here right now* is all there is, or that you were created by a Creator, or that life is meaningless, or that there is something bigger going on than what you can see--everybody has faith in something.
It's not an issue of having or not having faith, it's what you put your faith in.

You can choose to put your faith in whatever you want. That's part of this whole thing.

Nobody can force you to believe anything.
That's the beautiful part. You get to choose.

I choose the Bible. Not because I'm fake, or
pretending to be perfect, or overall
unintelligent. Not because it's some kind of a
crutch or I am bored, but because deep down
I'm a person who mostly feels crazy, and
insecure, and is angry, and flawed, and
severely confused, and stirring on the inside
with all these thoughts, and the Bible has a lot
to say about people who are like me--people
who have a God who is for them.

The story of the Bible is a story of a God who
is for people.
And a mystery of how everything is wound up
with love.

I put faith in the Bible because I want to see
more creativity, and exploration, and art, and
justice for people who are on the outside,
underdogs, or poor, or lost, or abandoned, or
frustrated by how those in power treat those
who aren't.

That's the story of the Bible, a God who
doesn't give up on people.

I'm one of those people.

You were created by God for him and his joy of having you around. God likes having you around. Think about that for a second. You are not an accident God puts up with. When he created you he said, *the world is missing something--something it can't go on without.* God saw the world and saw it was missing you so he did something about it. Do you have a place in the world? Clearly God thinks so. Your purpose is to worship him. That's it.

Worship is loving a God who loves you with the way you live.

One of the writers in the Bible, Paul, he says it this way:

"For we are God's masterpiece. He has created us anew in Christ Jesus, so we can do the good things he planned for us long ago."
You are a masterpiece.

The Bible isn't a list of answers.
If anything it's just the beginning of more questions.
Great things lead to more questions.

I've watched my parents. They are married still. Which I know is rare. They love each other. Not in an endless romantic comedy way. In a way that says I will be patient, I will be kind when you are obnoxious, I will serve you. My dad loves my mom in a way that says, when you throw up on the carpet, and you go to clean it up and you keep throwing up because you hate throw up, I'll tell you to go lay down and clean it up myself. That's love. Not flowers and cards. But actions. Love is a verb. Love does something.

My parents have a relationship where there are not more answers. Their marriage isn't a cheat sheet for life. They are so endlessly curious about each other, about how the other thinks, and what they will do, and how they can serve each other that it draws them into the next day. It's almost like the mystery of each other keeps them turning the page in their relationship.

This is what it's like with God. Once you think you have the whole thing figured out, you've missed everything. Grace is a mystery. The cross is a mystery. Love is endlessly exploring patience, kindness, and self-control.

I grew up going to a church as a kid. The one memory I can clearly see is I remember getting pantsed outside the sanctuary by a bulky kid with a raging bull-cut named Christopher, who was a few years older than me. I didn't know pantsing was a thing. I had never been pantsed or seen anybody pantsed. I just knew one moment I was strolling pleasantly in a single-file line during Sunday school on the way to our classroom, and the next my scrawny legs were very cold, and my cargo pants were snug around my ankles and there was amplified laughter from all sides of the walkway. I hated that moment. I still hate thinking about it. I didn't know what to be embarrassed about. I wasn't embarrassed about people seeing my underwear. I ran around in my underwear all the time (I still do, it's underwear people get over it). I wasn't embarrassed because Christopher yanked my pants down in one fell swoop, *who cares*. I was embarrassed because everybody had stopped, right there, to make me feel like a dingle-weed. The line had halted to point and giggle at my shame. If I had been pantsed and nobody laughed I would have walked away without a scar.

This wasn't just a pantsing, it was a public shaming.

Christopher could have simply ruffled my hair, and if everybody had paused to laugh, I'd still have been mortified.

Did I like going to church? Not really. It felt like a bunch of bullies. Not just Christopher, but others too, who thought because they followed the rules and said the right stuff that they had it figured out.

Some of us just stand there at church, knowing we aren't good enough, feeling heavy with shame, several embarrassed with our pants around our ankles, wishing it would all just be over.

For a while my parents let me stay in the mini-van parked out in the parking lot while they churched it up without me. I don't know how I worked this deal but I was *supposed* to read my Bible while I sat there.
That's where I stumbled into Jesus.

In the story of Jesus, he spends a lot of time sticking up for people bullied by religious people or people with a bunch of rules on how to get to God. He spends most his time with outcasts and sinners and well, people like me. He said this one thing that stuck with me, where his way of loving and learning and seeing God is light and not heavy. It's simple.

This didn't sound like religion to me, sitting in that stuffy back seat of our family mini-van, it sounded like a new way to live.

Early followers of Jesus called the whole thing they were a part of "The Way".

They thought it was simple.

It was so simple in fact that onlookers saw these people following Jesus and said, "this isn't even a religion," they looked at how they lived and said, "there's no temple or sacrifices or list of rules."

And these followers of Jesus were like, "We know, because it's all about Jesus. He's the temple, the sacrifice, and the rules."

It wasn't a new religion. It wasn't a new list of rules. It wasn't a bunch of ridiculous superstition, or meaningless garbage. It was a way of seeing the world all around you. A way of living where you begin to realize God is doing things all around and in everything, and isn't inside some temple, or shrine, or altar, but was right there with you and all of creation. The Way was seeing what God had been doing the whole time and joining in. The Way was God inviting me and you into the mystery.

We get to play a part.

I knew that this changed everything. It was my own personal Renaissance. I went from a stale, burdened, limited view of faith to something erupting with inspiration and a better story. Everybody needs their own personal Renaissance, where they go from the Dark Ages to endless imagination. Where everything around you begins to light up and you realize God's holiness isn't something to be protected, but is contagious. I think it's what Jesus meant when he went around telling people to turn around and begin something new because the Kingdom of God was here.

I believe this way is a better way to be human.

I believe that forgiveness is a better way to live.

I believe giving is a better way to live.

I believe serving others is a better way to live.

I believe exploring the Bible is a better way to live.

———————

Back to Jacob, out in the middle of nowhere face-to-face with his creator. He's pissed off. He's spent a lot of time with himself as the center of his universe. He decides to wrestle God. Here's the thing about Jacob: he's running from his past. Ever feel like you're running from a past you'd rather forget?

His whole life has been an attempt at knowing deep in his bones that he's loved.

His name literally means *grabber*. We'll grab at anything around us when we feel empty of any love.

Jacob is tangled up in insecurities, anxiety, and anger.

His family is a mess. He cheats his brother of his blessing while his father is on his deathbed. When you don't feel loved, you'll do anything to feel blessed. Lie, cheat, fight, steal, smoke, snort, sleep around, binge, blackout, cut, curse--anything to feel less empty. And none of it works.

Anything to feel blessed.
Anything to feel *anything*.

He's on the run from a brother who hates his guts. His life is one mistake after another. He got screwed over by his father-in-law and he's exhausted, alone in this desert wilderness.

In the middle of nowhere. He can't sleep. He's too restless to unwind. Tired of running. Wishing for a home that doesn't exist.

His past chasing him.

Somewhere in the midst of this, he meets God.

Have you ever felt backed into a wall? Ever felt like you'd do anything to feel loved? Ever stopped sleeping? God always meets us when we are restless, lost, and have nothing left. Jacob wrestles God right there on the side of the road in the dead of night until the sun comes up.

I don't know what your past is like. I don't know what anxiety you carry on your shoulders or who has hurt you. I don't know what your wilderness is or where you feel unloved.

It took standing there with all those kids pointing and laughing for me to sit in that minivan and experience Jesus. It took wrestling God, and putting myself into the orbit I belonged in all along. Worship is realizing you orbit around God, not vise-versa.

I know we all wrestle with God.

And that's okay.

Because I don't believe in a God who's far away, but a God who will get dirty and who will let us wrestle. Who embraces our pain. Who sees where we are empty.

Jacob won't let go until God blesses him.

And right there, God blesses him.

But it wasn't about God blessing Jacob, Jacob was always blessed, he just had never realized it. But it took wrestling. It took some running. It took a whole journey before Jacob realized what was there all along.

That he was loved.

HOLD YOUR FIRE
FEBRUARY, *JUNIOR YEAR OF HIGH SCHOOL*

"It's a lot harder to find a submachine gun than you'd think," I say as we drive out of the school parking lot.

"Who knew?" Blake says, pressing hard against the gas pedal, whipping past all our classmates climbing into cars with the marks of exhaustion plastered all over their faces. February in Seattle is a blanket of cold rain that can seriously suck the life out of you. An unrelenting fury. Every morning you get up in total darkness, the world covered by a heavy, grey cloud--you don't see sunlight until halfway through first period, and even then, it's submerged within the grey expanse. From the windows of my school the evergreen trees outside reverberate with the wind and rain. By the time you leave school it's dark again. Everybody is living in a cloud. Faces look pale, sleepy, and a little sad from the lack of sunlight.

I've called Blake my best friend since preschool. There's a picture in some box somewhere of us at swimming lessons as scrawny four-year-olds clutching our elbows cross-armed and shivering at the edge of the community pool.

The thing about Blake and I being best friends is that it's far less volatile as most best-friendness, because basically at some point in early elementary school we looked at each other and said, 'yeah best friends for life.'

There was really no going back.

We don't find a new best friend. We don't best friend break up. We don't have eyes for any other best friend. Okay, this is starting to get weird--you get it.

"Right or left?" he says, drifting to the stop sign just beyond the student lot.

"I thought a submachine gun would be a standard thing people would have," I say, reaching for a stack of cassette tapes scattered on the floor. Blake and I, we've decided that cassette tapes are the new thing. Forget your fancy digital music. It's all about the squeaky whine of cassette tapes. Blake's dad got him this old-school Cadillac that only has a cassette player anyway so it kind of forced our hand. Our afternoons are filled with hunting through Goodwill and antique shops for the music we like--Bob Dylan, Ray

Charles, Nina Simone, and Simon and Garfunkel.

I pick one towards the top, *Elton John*. I should have guessed. Blake was lucky, his dad had these boxes of his cassette collection in the garage. It was mostly Sir Elton John but there were also some rare gems. Zeppelin. Earth Wind and Fire. Johnny Cash. Even some later stuff--The Clash. The Smiths. Red Hot Chili Peppers. *Freaking Blake and his awesome dad.*

"I'd buy one," I say, sliding the tape into the mouth of the dashboard. "I mean, I'd rather rent a submachine gun because it's really only one night that I need it for." The cassette player growled and murmured before piano keys came rolling through the speakers.

"Right or left?!"

"Right... NO! NO! Left. My right."

"We're sitting the same direction! Right or left?"

"Left, sorry, left for sure."

The wide body of the Cadillac, or *Cady* as Blake calls her, crosses the dashed yellow line, quietly accelerating. We pass the lineup of students lugging bulky backpacks walking home.

———

Anna Sofia and I are going to Tolo together. She asked me in the parking lot on a Friday after I got back to school from being sick. I don't know what I expected. She came up behind me, tapped me on the shoulder, "BL, you and me--Tolo? What's your thoughts?" I probably said that I thought it would be the best thing ever too quickly. The really slick, ladies-men, polo-shirt wearing guys always do this pause--they pause as if they have this plethora of options and need a moment to really process.

That is what those guys do. What I did looks something like:

Anna Sofia:
BL, you and me-- T...

Brain:
Cool it dude... I know it sounds like she's going to say Tolo. Like the dance. But she's not. She's for sure not. Let her finish her sentence before you make any sort of facial reaction.

Me:
Too late. (smiles like a homeschooler at
Legoland)

Brain:
You look like the kid in the pool who's peeing
with that dumb grin on your face.

Me:
I can't help it. You know why?

Brain:
Why?

Me:
Cause she's asking me to Tolo. What now
sucka!

Brain:
She's not.

Me:
She is and I'm going to say "YES". Right now.

Brain:
She's not done talking.

Me:
Really? This whole talking back and forth has
taken a long time.

Brain:
It really hasn't--your thoughts travel at 120 miles per second.

Me: Oh.

Brain:
She's still hallway through her sentence.

Me:
(To Anna)
YES!

Anna Sofia:
…olo? What's your thoughts?
(Pauses because I shouted right in her ear hallway through her sentence)

Me:
(To my Brain)
Did that come off too strong?

Brain:
You basically reek of desperation. It's beyond pathetic.

Me:
But she did ask me. Told you so.

Brain:
Lower your voice Bryan. She probably thinks
you have a mental disorder.

Me:
Or that I'm stoked for Tolo and so I projected
my inner excitement through expression.

Brain:
I get it. You got me working overtime up here,
you're thinking about her so much. You've got
to get a hold of yourself.
Me:
I am fine. I am just in high school--it's what
you do. It just happens.

Brain:
Negatory captain. That's what you want to tell
yourself. You have more control than you
think. I know--I work up here. You don't.

Me:
I like her. I am going to this dance.

Brain:
Out of all the bodies and souls, I got stuck
with your crazy self.

Me:
I'm not crazy.

Brain:
I don't exist. I'm a projection of your inner thoughts as you talk to yourself. That's textbook crazy.

Me:
Argh, you are right.

Tolo is a themed dance where high-schoolers are encouraged to choose a costume theme portraying a famous couple from fiction or real-life. Anna and I chose the bank robbing, original gangster couple Bonnie and Clyde. I had already found the pin-stripe suit and pinch hat, now I just need one of those Tommy Guns. There's a party rental store I called that says they have it.

"I only got one," the guy on the phone protests, "so you better hurry."
As if there is high demand on plastic toy submachine gun rentals during the month of February. Still, I figure better safe than a submachine gun-less Tolo, so Blake and I race over straight after sixth period Chemistry.

The party rental store isn't a store at all. I'll use the word *garage* loosely because *tin shack* might be more appropriate. It's not in a bad area *per se*, but it's definitely not an area you normally go to.

It's not far from our school, about a quarter of a mile into the woods. There's a pizza place, a computer repair store, and a Frisbee Golf course. The whole area is sketchy. There was a rumor going around for a while that a group of teenagers were living in the woods like Lord of the Flies. My friend Max said he saw them. He said they tried to steal his dog once. I don't know if that's true, but I wouldn't have been surprised.

One time Blake and I went with Max's older brother into the woods. He was three or four years older and way cooler. He kept telling us we were going to *freak out* when he showed us what he'd drug us to.

"Dead body?" I whispered to Blake as we trailed behind.

"Or maybe a séance?" He replied.

"Crap," I shook my head repeatedly, "I sure hope not, I got stuff to do."

There were also rumors of strange rituals happening late in the night in these woods-- like some straight-up Harry Potter freaky stuff going down--stories of people getting weird, starting giant fires, running around naked, dancing around in circles and stealing people's dogs. I don't think these rumors had any truth. But it was the kind of stuff that totally freaks me out. I told myself they were probably just rumors, but I wasn't looking to take any chances. I am not a scary movie kind of guy. I'm just not. I don't get scared--I get bothered. Life can be dark enough- why go looking for evil? It might just be me but I don't go sniffing out that kind of stuff. I thought about these dog stealing, wild, naked, teenagers dancing around fires as we stomped through dead leaves and swatted tree branches out of our face. *What a horrible place to be naked,* I thought as I attempted to dodge sticker bushes, inevitably getting my sweatshirt stuck and spinning to get free. Still, I played tough as we marched on. I puffed out my chest and said really brave stuff like, "I'm not afraid of anything... ever!"

That's what brave people say *right*? I don't actually know.

"We're here," came a voice from the front of the group.

I stepped up towards everybody staring at the same thing, and it wasn't what I was thinking. Not even close.

An empty motel pool, clearly abandoned-- splotched rust, an orange residue running down the sides, wet leaves, pine needles, and trash. It was the standard, watermelon-shaped, teal painted pool with white short stairs leading into a shallow end that gradually grew deeper with little bold numbers indicating depth.

The walls had a little 12 marked at the deepest point. A small drain marked the center. Our jaws dropped.

If an empty motel pool doesn't explode your heart with joy--you aren't a skater.

A hidden, empty pool is a legendary myth to all skateboarders. It's the Holy Grail. El Dorado. The Fountain of Youth. You might spend your whole life searching. It's Ahab's white whale. It's what you drool over in skate magazines. It's the very treasure you dream of stumbling into. Skate-parks are too crowded. The mall, or sidewalks, or public staircases had security guards. This place could be ours. Our secret swimming pool out in the middle of the woods.

The only downside- it was trashed from years of damage and overgrowth. There were scattered beer cans, newspaper, crumpled up plastic bags.

It smelt like mildew.

Over the course of the next few weeks, we planned cleaning parties--we'd never been so organized in our life. We swept and scrubbed. Brought in an old couch. After school we'd trek over and skate for hours. It was ours. All ours.

There are places in our life we don't want to go. Sometimes it's what we hold too tight to. It's unforgiveness or something in life we think matters that really doesn't. I think Jesus is always leading us into these places we want to avoid so we can become more like him. We have to step out of our comfort zone. There's usually some cleanup involved. It's always a process, but out of it we grow. Our faith grows. What was once just woods becomes adventure. What was once a dirty, abandoned pool full of pine needles became our very own skate spot.

Jesus sees our lives full of unleashed potential. Where we see nothing, Jesus sees everything. He does it over and over in the gospels. There's a fisherman named Peter. Jesus walks up to Peter, just standing there on this beach and he's like, "Peter, listen, stop fishing--put down the nets you've used your whole life--we're going to go do something new, I'm going to teach you to fish for people." Jesus sees what Peter is great at and says, "I want to use that to bless the whole world."

I used to think Jesus wanted to turn me into somebody I wasn't. There was something about the empty pool that made me realize Jesus wanted to change my purpose so I could become more of myself.

The crazy thing is, Peter, right there on that beach drops his net and follows Jesus. He knows there is more to his life than just fishing. Does it take work? Yes. Is it a process? Of course. But the payoff of Peter embarking on Jesus' mission is worth it.

My guess is Peter never looked back to those nets on the beach. My guess is, for Peter, everything had possibility.

"Are you sure this is the right place?" Blake opens his door, inching his head out of the window, "there's no sign."

I say I think so, that this is the right address. I am looking around at the gravel parking lot and the white metal garage. I open the door to a dark warehouse with mostly Christmas decorations--which I think is strange, because who *rents* their Christmas decorations? Towards the back are Halloween costumes. The front is filled with cheap wedding props--

fake flowers, gold candle holders, columns, and glass vases.

The clerk at the front desk hands me my toy submachine gun. I sign a rental agreement and pay the fee with cash.

"I don't think I've ever seen you take a dance this serious," Blake says, walking back to the car.

"I don't know," I say. "This one feels different."

WELCOME HOME
TEN YEARS AFTER JUNIOR YEAR OF HIGH
SCHOOL

You know those inkblot tests? The ones that
fold down the middle, creating those
symmetrical stains that looks like a pen
explosion? The ones psychologists use to
analyze the subconscious of patients? The
blots are marked by different sizes and
shapes and typically look like a bat with their
wings stretched to the edge of the page.
Psychologists call them Rorschach tests, and
they're used, among other things, to analyze
the perceptions of underlying thoughts.

There is something about inkblots that tell you
something about yourself. About how you see
things around you. About how you see
yourself. About how you see the world. You
project the mess inside you onto the mess on
the page. There are a million things you can
see. There are a million right answers. But at
its core, it isn't about the splattered ink, or
about your response, or even what you see--
it's about what's happening inside of you. It's
about answering the splatters, the inkblots
inside your own head.

By analyzing the blots they can help untangle the knots tied up in you.
The church is the same way.
It's an inkblot.

The church is made up of people. It isn't a building. It isn't a service or gathering. The church has no demographic; no zip code, no genre, no particular political agenda, and no social class. It's people.

What we are describing when we use a word like "church" is people. If a particular church feels uninspired, it's because the people are uninspired. If your hour-long Sunday service filled with the typical stand, sit, worship, listen, read, and leave feels stifling and cliché--it's a reflection of the people. It's one giant inkblot.

Jesus said he would build his church and the powers of hell, of death, of hopelessness, of all chaos wouldn't be able to put up a fight against it.

What Jesus was talking about doesn't sound boring.
It doesn't sound like a Sunday morning thing.
It sounds like an all the time thing.
The church Jesus spoke of was built on the breath of the Holy Spirit, on uprooting culture, on this new creation, this new kingdom that was breaking in and stepping toe-to-toe with

the power of Rome and pagan culture and the grip of death itself. This was the Messiah. Rebuilding the temple in three days. This was the Savior entering enemy territory, snatching the keys to hell and setting captives free.

This was a movement.
And Jesus invited people along with him.

But this wasn't a new culture. This was the culture all along. This is what God the Father had been talking about the whole time. From the beginning, God's new creation was a story of new humanity. The Exodus, the wilderness, the Promised Land, the temple, these were all just the workings of this counterculture. This kingdom which John the Baptist ushers in and Jesus fulfills, it's precisely the way things were meant to be. From the first steps in the Garden, to the waves Noah sails, to the songs of David and the empty tomb on the third day, this was the movement God was leading us into. Everything else was a sham in comparison. Egypt was a sham, Caesar was a sham, Rome was a sham and Satan himself was a sham, all in comparison to God's upside down cultural revolution.

The thing about inkblots is that they point to a deeper need. They aren't the diagnosis, the prescription, or the medication. The church isn't any of these, either. It's people--reflecting what God is doing in his creation.

It's people on the mission with Jesus to help heal the world.
So what happens when that reflection gets blurry? When it gets all fogged up with a bunch of other stuff? When you don't like what you see?

Jesus comments a lot on a blurry reflection of God's people. It was the crisis all around him. The tension of Jesus' day was that of, 'what exactly was God up to?' What happens when you are God's chosen people but you don't feel chosen any longer? What happens when you are longing for new but you can't seem to break out of the old? When the old ways of thinking don't seem to be working and the questions of what could be next don't seem to have very clear answers.

In the book of Exodus, which can be considered the starting point of the story of the Bible, we see God dive into the mess and rescue his people from slavery in the mega-empire of Egypt. He leads them, and they follow into the wilderness and to a land he had vowed would be their home. Home is a concept God puts on the top of his priority list throughout the entire Bible. This home would be a land flowing with milk and honey, which was an ancient Jewish way of saying this place would be a paradise--referencing the paradise God had intended from the beginning. This was the original home. He would be their God and they would be his people. That was the plan. God was doing the unthinkable. He was on the move--rescuing, pursuing and redeeming.

Right there, in the wilderness, en route to this new home, God sets up rules of engagement--which in those days would have read as wedding vows--for his people through the Ten Commandments. Guidelines of how exactly this relationship would work. God isn't meeting with his people in a temple, or in a service, he's with them on a journey. He meets with his people for the first time right smack-dab in the middle of nowhere, on a mountain, in the middle of this adventure.

Again and again we see God's people break this bond. They decimate the vows. Break the covenant. They cheat on the God who rescued them.

In Jesus' generation, the thought was that what Israel really needed was a second Exodus. God moving in a new way, to free his people--not only politically from Rome, but also in a full and final swoop to the entire world.

Jesus, hassled endlessly by the religious authorities of the day, makes the comment:

"No one ever pours new wine into old leather bags. Otherwise, the new wine will break the bags, the wine will spill out, and the leather bags will be ruined."

Jesus' mission is initiating a huge dose of 'new'. New community, new ways of thinking, new creation, but all of this needs a whole new context.

God is new wine. He's always been new wine. Most of the Bible--Old and New Testament--is this story about how 'new wine' God really is. He's constantly in the margin of thought, creativity, morality, and bandwidth for compassion, and he's inviting his creation to join him there. Which is kind of a funny thing, because how often do we make God out to be this old-fashioned, archaic, outdated, intolerant character? God in our culture is known for shutting the party down. He's stomping into our world, arms crossed.

But that's not the God we see in the story of his people. *That* God hears *too far gone* and thinks *nope, not yet. That* God breathes life into *too far gone*. He sees the framework, the box, the contexts we build to put him in, and says *yes, and even more than that.*

Jesus gives the radical example of a shepherd watching ninety-nine sheep and leaving the flock to rescue the one that is *too far gone.*

This is Jesus bursting right through the old. We get caught up thinking the opposite, that we're the new wine and God's the old, decrepit wine skin. But Jesus turns the table back on us. The story of God is a story of humanity, following God into something greater than where we just were.

From the beginning God's purpose was to see his creation grow. He created a garden for his guy Adam to seriously go nuts in. It was a place of adventure. But it wasn't done, it wasn't finished the way we think of finished. We were given a position in this creation. We were, from the start of the story, given a post in the business of naming creation.

Is there anything more personal, more *intimate* than giving something a name?

Think of farm animals. You don't name the ones you are going to turn into a meat-lovers pizza. If you have a chicken, all you see is grilled chicken enchiladas. Until somebody goes around and messes it all up and names that chicken Mike. Now that bird that's pecking and clucking around the yard isn't just a future

dinner, it's Mike. How can you kill Mike?
Seriously, how you gonna do Mike like that?

God gives us authority, and with that comes
the opportunity to tend and watch over the
garden he has grown. A place that God
himself has blessed and called holy. There,
God gives us the mission of naming and
creating a culture.

I don't know about you, but that sounds like a
mission I can believe in.
Here's what I know about people. We know
the world is messed up and deep down we
want to help. We know bullying is wrong. We
know our families are jacked up. We know
judging others sucks. We know nobody should
feel like suicide is their only option. We know
that things are broken.

You say, "somebody should do something
about all this."
God's like, "that's why I sent you."

The church is God's way of saying, "let's do
something about this."

God allowed his creation the opportunity to
creatively invest in the creative process. We
get to give identity to the world around us.
Creation reflects the Creator, and we get to
invent, organize, and construct the creation

around us. We are a part of the creative growth.

At eight years old my mom gave me an outrageous opportunity. She looked at how much I like drawing pictures. I was homeschooled and had a lot of extra time so she got me paint and a brush and said that I got to paint my room. And not just like: this wall's going to be red and this one's going to be blue, but I got to sketch waves and cartoon surfers along all the walls. I painted a sun around the light on my ceiling. There were little surfers riding, crashing, and jumping on the rolling waves wrapped around the once blank walls. That wasn't just a room in a house. That wasn't just a room I slept in and kept my things in. No, that was *my* room.

God breathed into us and saw that it was good. He saw our creativity. He saw our whole life. He saw how much we wanted to be a part of this creation. He handed us a paintbrush and a bucket of color and said, *let's make this happen.*
The church is you with a paintbrush in hand.

How often do we miss this? How often do we settle for feeling uninspired? We get our hearts broken or we hurt somebody or somebody hurts us, or we stop growing, or we feel anxious, or guilty, or we get stuck in a pattern or addiction and we get calloused. We turn into skeptics. The writer of the book of Revelation, the final book in the Bible, gives us one of the most assured declarations in the whole story of the Bible: the writer John sees a new heaven and new earth. And this old earth--this place where sadness, loneliness, hurt, bitterness, evil, and sin has had its day and been officially defeated--it totally disappears and there is this loud shout, like this hope-filled, passionate, inspired announcement:

"God's home is now among his people!"

And this voice, this voice that began the story by commanding light into the universe, which spoke us into existence, this voice that ushered in Creation, says:

"I am making all things new."

We get to be a part of this 'new'. We get to be a part of something bigger than ourselves. God won't ever stop leading us further into this place with him. He's always finding blank places and handing us paint buckets.

But what happens when we forget? When we dismiss our God-given creativity? Or worse, we put down the brush and stop painting? What happens when we stop projecting our creative identity onto creation? What happens when we stop loving and caring for others? What happens when the church stops being the church?

"When two or more people get together," Jesus says, "I'll be with them."

Jesus says when you meet with another person and you love like he does, that's a church. When people tell me what church they wish they had, I usually tell them to *be* that church. Become that church. Go start it. Sit in the lunchroom and start that thing. Go feed the homeless. Go start a group that talks about the Bible. Start a band. Not a Christian band, but a really great band and then talk about all the stuff Jesus talks about. You don't have to go preach to people or smack them with a Bible, you can just live as Jesus lived and let the Holy Spirit do the rest. Don't try and stuff Jesus down people's throats, he won't fit. Love people, really love them, especially when you hate them. Forgive enemies. Read to old people. Stop sex trafficking. Eat dinner with your parents even when they drive you crazy. Ask questions. Serve your parents, even when they are the worst. Be okay with messy. Jesus can work with messy better than he works with pretend perfect.

When you are wrong, admit you are wrong. Stop being a victim--you are not a victim, really sucky stuff happened to you, a lot of it still hurts--you are not a victim, you are a new creation in Christ; leave being a victim at the door. Don't blame others. Forgive your dad. Listen and love people who are different than you and fight for them. Stand up against bullying. All bullying, especially the bullying you are a part of. Admit that the church is imperfect people. Love radically. Care about people. Start that thing. You and a friend. You and five friends. You and a hundred friends.

Grab a Bible and invite friends at the lunch table. Read what Jesus says and talk about it. Invite outcasts. Invite that kid nobody likes. Invite that kid over there and his girlfriend. Invite the people who eat alone. Invite the stoners. Invite the ASB president. Invite the gamers. Invite the cool girls. You have a church.

"And all the believers met together in one place," the writer of Acts says, "and shared everything they had. They sold their property and possessions and shared the money with those in need."

This is a picture of the church: a group of people meeting together and sharing what they have. It goes on to say:

"And each day the Lord added to their fellowship those who were being saved."

The church is a place where everybody has a place. Where those who are lost are found. Where you have a home. Where you celebrate a new life found in Christ. You don't have a church--you are the church. A church is a place where you grow. You realize how selfish you are and begin to see what it means to be the real you.

Here's what the church isn't: a place that says I told you so.

The church is a place where it's safe to say:

My heart is messy,
My soul is selfish,
My brain is busted,
My life is lacking,
And I need a savior.

What I love about the church is it isn't just about you. Or me. It's about forgiving others. It's about eating food together. It's about realizing you don't need to live with a lot, but can live with a little and give a lot to others who need it. It's about admitting you are addicted to pornography, or money, or control, or hurting yourself, or success and you move forward. Not with your own strength, but with

Jesus and the power of the Holy Spirit. As Paul says in 2 Corinthians:
"My grace is all you need. My power works best in weakness."

So now I am glad to boast about my weaknesses, so that the power of Christ can work through me. I've seen it. I've experienced it and it's powerful. I hope you get to as well.

One writer in the Psalms says:

"Taste and see that the Lord is good."

If you have a place in your soul that longs to be with people who want to live fully, and to worship God by loving others, and to give generously, and you haven't found it yet it's because God has called you to be it.

Go, start it.
That's the church.
And Jesus said he'd be there with you.

SEATTLE ON A SCHOOL NIGHT
FEBRUARY, *JUNIOR YEAR OF HIGH SCHOOL*

The tickets online are $40 a piece, not including tax. I am seventeen years old, but I don't totally understand how sales tax works the way I probably should. I was homeschooled, give me a break. We spent most of our time learning about how to make tea out of pinecones and how to milk goats-- two things that have not helped me get a girlfriend. I know I need at least ten to twenty extra dollars for tax, but who knows--I don't even know if the government knows. I have a $100 check from my grandma from Christmas. Not because I'm good at saving, but because I lost it and recently hunted in my bedroom for several days to find it. If I couldn't find it, there was no way a criminal could either, so that's something. My security system works. On second thought maybe I am really good at saving, my techniques are just advanced. Anyway, I have this $100 check and I need to get two tickets.

"Bryan, the concert is on a school night," My mom says from the kitchen. "You know you can't go to a concert on a school night."

Brain:
Is that true? I can't find any memories on that one.

Me:
I don't know. I don't think I've ever tried. I'm really testing what I can and cannot do on this one. But I have to go.

Brain:
You just need a strong case.

Me:
I know I do, but I need the right angle or I'll get shut down.

Brain:
Guilt trip?

Me:
No, too predictable. I need something better.

Brain:
Flattery?

Me:
She'll catch on that I want something.

Brain:
Here's what I say, line up your case--let her know you have it all planned out, then plop on a little "wouldn't you want a nice guy like me to

take you on a date when you were Anna's age?"

Me:
Got it.

"This would be a one-time thing," I say, still scrolling through ticket prices. "I have the money. I just need to put it on your credit card. You can keep the check, I'll give you the extra $20 as a thank you for the whole no concerts on a school night thing."

My mom gives me a half smile.

I'm making headway.

"I don't know. Seattle at night, I just don't think it sounds safe."

It isn't safe. But it's not dangerous. We live on the other side of a body of water from Seattle. To get to the city you ride a ferryboat. It's a half hour ride and then you are in downtown Seattle. All I'm asking is that she lets Anna and I go to this concert a couple blocks from the ferry on a Thursday night. We'd see the indie band Bright Eyes at the Paramount Theater.

"Mom," I say emphatically, looking straight at her. "Think about you at Anna's age, didn't you want a nice boy like me to buy you concert tickets on a school night just to show how much he liked you? Wouldn't that have been cool? Don't shoot me down here."

She laughs a little and keeps quickly preparing dinner.

"Just let me live mom! Let me see the world! I want to LIVE!"

Me:
I realize I'm laying it on kinda thick, but I think we've got this.

Brain:
Is all of this worth it?

Me:
I just want to take her on a date and you keep making me second-guess myself.
Brain:
I'm just asking.

Me:
This is exhausting. I don't want to have to convince you and my mom.

Brain:
Listen, I just don't think you need a girlfriend. I'm serious, it's a mess in here. I don't know how you can expect to support another human

being until you get some stuff figured out in here. I'll be honest too, I know you think you're emotionally stable and basically have the world figured out but you're running on about half the bandwidth you will eventually be running on. Here's my suggestion: sit down and get some things in order before dating this girl, or any girl. Get your classes in better shape. Maybe learn how to cook. Try some new things. Read those books you've always wanted to read.

Me:
You want me to have no friends and no love life. Perfect. I thought you were on my side.

Brain:
I am. Trust me- I am. I want to see you healthy and happy. That's all I want. I just don't think this is the right thing.

"Bryan? Bryan?" my mom says as she taps my shoulder. "Stop doing that thing where you zone out. I said you could go. It's fine. But just this once, and you have to make sure it's okay with her parents. I don't want to get a call from her mom, mad 'cause I let her daughter go to a concert on a school night."

Boom.

Me:
That's how it's done son.
Brain:
Congratulations.

I enter the credit card information and click purchase. I am the only guy I know who is doing what I'm doing. This is new territory. I'm an innovator. A pioneer. I'm taking a girl to an indie concert in Seattle on a frickin' school night.

I imagine the face she'll make when I give her the ticket. When I ask her to go with me. When I tell her it's on a school night. When I pick her up and when we get on a ferryboat. The insides of me are doing handsprings and playing mariachi music. My heart is applauding my triumph.

"Just be careful," my mom says, placing a plate of spaghetti in front of the laptop. "And don't do anything stupid."

The next night I have a plan set into motion for the tickets. I go to her house casually, saying we should watch television. She won't suspect a thing, except I actually say the word 'television' on the phone because I'm nervous, making me sound either old or creepy and I regret saying it. Still, I'm pretty sure she isn't on to me. I go over to her house. For a while we sit on stools in her kitchen talking to her dad who tells me about all the paintings in the house of old wooden boats and where he got them. I nod and smile. Some of the paintings are lit from small lights above, making them look like the ones out of a museum. He tells me about dates, and artist names, and the engineering of particular boats to which I nod and say things back like, "fascinating" and "stunning" and "wonderful work".

Nobody suspects a thing.

Next, we aimlessly skip through sitcom shows trying to find something watchable, but mostly making fun of the characters' neck fat. After a few hours I confess that I have to go home to finish homework. She walks me to the front door. I give her a hug. She says she'll see me tomorrow.
Go time!

After the door closes and she's gone back inside, I do unnecessary ninja moves along the cobblestone walkway lined with rhododendrons. This is because I am pumped. Also, because I am a ninja and ninja moves are awesome.

I get in my car and swat away the balloons that fill every inch of the inside of my car. Yes, balloons. Lots of them.

At the end of her driveway I stop, headlights on, and get out of my car. The thick trees lining her driveway protect me from being seen.

Here I place a large homemade sign standing on two large orange cones right in the center of her driveway where it meets the main road, pointing toward her house. Painted on the sign in big bold letters it says, "Bright Eyes for your beautiful eyes." It's cheesy, really cheesy, I know. I realize this as I place it in the cones. I stand staring at the sign for a second. It sounded great when I wrote it. I don't have time to second-guess it now. Balloons are being tied to the cones. Candy sprinkled on the ground. No, *no* the candy is too much. I stop. It looks like a seven-year-old's birthday party. I slowly pick up each individual piece of candy and put them back in my car, except a Snickers, which I stuff in my mouth immediately.

I gaze at my glorious creation.

For the cherry on top, I put her ticket in an envelope and tape it to the sign.

Boom.

———————

At school the next day she gives me a big hug. She's carrying around one of the balloons. My balloons. The balloons I picked out from the party store and had the clerk fill with helium. Anna is carrying it around the halls of school telling everybody the story. My sign is becoming legendary. I walk by groups of girls who giggle or say things like "way to raise the bar Bryan!"

Anna tells me she asked her parents and they're totally cool with it. She tells me she knows a burger place just down the street we can walk to. She says they have amazing burgers. She says when she was a little girl, they lived in Seattle and her dad would take her there all the time. She says we have to get milkshakes.

My stomach is doing the whole handspring, mariachi music thing again.

We're having a conversation involving her childhood. That's sweet. Childhood nostalgic reflections are a giant leap in a relationship. Oh *shoot*. Did I just say relationship? I'm getting ahead of myself. Clearly.

But still, she's taking me to her favorite childhood burger spot. That's pretty awesome.

On the ferry ride over we stay in the car, watching the wide ocean splash against the side of the boat. We watch the houses move by and point at the ones we'd like to live in one day. Mine tend to be modern and cubed with simple cement shapes. Hers are cabins, small and hidden behind mansions.

The evening is pale grey with clouds, but it does not rain. Seagulls float alongside the boat, catching the French fries of tourists. We see the city off on the horizon. The Space Needle's iconic UFO--shaped face, the sprawl of skyscrapers against an overcast sky, the piers, and the long orange neck of industrial cranes resting over massive container ships in port beside rows of stacked multicolor metal containers.

I've never driven in the city and my hands feel clammy against the steering wheel as I put the car into drive and we crawl off the ferry, merging into afternoon commuter traffic. We turn up a street so steep I feel like an astronaut preparing for launch. I'm sitting straight back. I can feel myself up against the fabric of the seat. My foot rests on the brake; we are locked in traffic. I'm going straight up into the sky. I look over at her.

She's sitting on the passenger seat with her legs tucked under herself and she's resting on the center console. Her Converse's poke out against the side door. She looks comfortable. Happy. I try and press pause. I try and stop time. To enjoy the right now. She's flipping through the radio. She's comfortable. Content. Oblivious to the world outside. We are going straight up. I can't see the top, only the lipstick--red brake lights of a cab in front of us. Businessmen in trench coats holding briefcases and tightly closed umbrellas walk on both sides of us. Cyclists speed past on the left. The buildings bloom on both sides of us. Reflective sheets of glass getting smaller as they ascend into the sky so far you have to press your face against the side of the car to see the top. Narrow alleys with shop clerks carrying bulky plastic garbage bags, smoking, yelling, and leaning against brick facades.

She wasn't lying about the burgers. They are messy, and greasy, and fall apart with every bite spilling their toppings into yellow wrappers. The French fries are different. Not bad different. Just unusual. They're skinny and stuck together in clumps. I like them the best. She orders a chocolate shake and I say I'll have the same. I pay. She says thank you. We sit on a curb to eat until rain starts to sprinkle so we move to the car. It rains harder. We look for parking. I can't parallel park. I don't know how. No, maybe I do. I'm not confident with her in the car, and in moving city streets that aren't patient or forgiving.

We find a parking garage. I spend twelve dollars. She says she'll pay me back. I say don't worry about it. 'It's on me' I say because that's what you say when you are really trying to say 'this is a date'. It's how you try, amongst all the mixed signals, to say you like her.

We are an hour and a half early. Neither of us has been to a concert in the middle of the city by ourselves. I am worried about being late. They let us inside because it's raining. Her hair looks pretty with rain in it. It's not wet. There is just the aftermath of running from the car to the door all over her hair. It's like the loose strands of her brown hair trapped a million tiny slivers of moisture. I save that picture of her in my head. It's the second picture of her I save from the night. By the end of the night there will be so many I will have to pick my favorites or forget them all. The building was built in the twenties and holds the beauty of a past era. There's expressive gold leaf décor and rich colors--tangerines and maroons and olives and deep splashes of blue. Chandeliers wilt from the ceiling giving the room an eternal glow.

I feel like we are from another century. It's just us. We convince somebody to let us in the auditorium early. Our seats are on the second balcony. We feel like aristocrats. High society of a long lost generation--a generation who sailed large oceans, and wrote letters in whimsical calligraphy, and knew the names of plants I can't pronounce, who memorized rather than recite, and knew how to really dance--not just grind and shake, but really dance. A generation of people who had dreams of a modern world we were now living in the reverberations of.

Our seats are right against the railing. It's the kind of show where you sit instead of stand. Her Converses beside my Vans. We sit alone, our stories filling the elegant theater. We explain all these moments that have gotten us here. Our history of ourselves. Puzzle pieces of who we are fitting together--upbringing, sports teams, family members, funny specifics, hidden talents, and rebellious tendencies, stretching over our short seventeen years. All these memories and opinions spilling out, intermingled and woven together, that have made up our lives.

A young man in a royal purple uniform shoos us out back into the hallway half an hour before the show. Final sound check he says. I ask him if he likes his job while he holds the door for us. I say it must be pretty cool. He merely shrugs and closes the door behind us. I buy a t-shirt. It's brown and says Bright Eyes in tiny letters. I don't like to wear brown. But I want to remember this. I want to have the t-shirt. Literally, the shirt could say, "I Eat Dirt" and I would still wear it. She gets popcorn. We go back in and sit back down. The room is crowded with people and it feels invasive. As though they are disturbing our now personal space, as if they've stormed into our living room. We feel like we own the place. Soon they all fade away.

It's a great show.

At one point in the middle of the set my brain tries to pipe in:

Brain:
She doesn't like you the way you think she does.

Me:
Shhh. Not right now, let me have this moment without you ruining it.

I look over--Anna is tapping the tops of her fingers against her thighs to the rhythm. A smile across her face. I've never seen her smile like this. I wonder if this is what that word *love* feels like. A thud of dizzying commotion inside. Do they say you *fall* in love because it's moments like this, moments where you feel like you can't go backwards, that you've lost control? I'm getting ahead of myself. But it could be? Love? Right? It has all the right symptoms. It was the first time I'd felt like *this.* Is this love? Do I love her? The lights are dim. A golden glow cast by the room. My Brain doesn't speak but I can sense it rolling its eyes. I steal a handful of popcorn, throwing it into my mouth. She turns to me and grabs my hand, curving her fingers between mine. From the stage way down below the band sings:

"We've been in between a past and future town.
We are nowhere and it's now."

PUTTING ON FLESH AND BLOOD
TEN YEARS AFTER JUNIOR YEAR OF HIGH SCHOOL

There's a word in the story of Jesus:

Incarnation.

It means God isn't far away.

In its Latin root form, "incarnation" literally means "to make into flesh", to become something made out of matter. To have atoms, molecules, flesh, blood, and everything that makes up a real thing. It means to become something you can touch.

For a long time in my life, faith wasn't a real thing.

It wasn't until Jesus became something real that my faith had:

Atoms,
Molecules,
Flesh,
And blood.

My grandpa was a pastor. He'd been a pastor since before I was born, so I never really saw him do all the things I thought pastors did--like stand in front of people and preach. I don't really remember him ever preaching to me or trying to get me to think a certain way. I do remember that he had this old black leather Bible. It was falling apart. There were scribbles, highlights, and shapes drawn in the margins like the diary of an explorer or scientist from centuries before.

That old black Bible sparked something inside me. I couldn't have been far from five years old, but I remember the feeling, a feeling that said:

"I want to explore too."

Mostly, I remember Christmas Eve. My sister and I would pile on the couch and he'd read us the story of Jesus being born. I can remember following his finger on the page as he read. I remember a sense of wonder. Of mystery. That inside this very old book held the unlocked potential of everything.

That my grandpa was letting us in on this incredible, creative, inspiring story that we got to be a part of.

Everybody wants to be a part of something bigger than themselves.

He'd say to us, right there on the couch, that this was a story about how God was taking back all of creation. That this story was about how we aren't alone. We didn't have to be afraid. We could be bold. God was going to rescue everything. This was a story of all these people waiting for a king, but that king came as a baby birthed by this teenage mom out in the middle of nowhere. That's where God chose to kick off the whole thing. Not in a temple, or with priests, or those who followed all the rules, but out in the middle of nowhere with outcasts. This wasn't a story about people doing all the right stuff, it was about a God who saw people who didn't feel good enough, or smart enough, or rich enough, or cool enough and said, "You're included in this really incredible thing I'm doing everywhere".

My grandpa, he'd close up his Bible with the binding falling apart, and lots of times right there he would sing. Just no shame, he'd hop right into song. He wasn't a guy afraid to sing. He'd start singing these old hymns and would sort of quietly let his voice fill the room.

The Christmas tree lit up. The presents placed underneath. The smell of his coffee.
Sometimes a few other family members would

pitch in with him and the room would come alive with voices, but other times--and these are the ones I remember the most--he'd just quietly sing to himself, closing the black leather Bible, and my sister and I, we'd listen to him sing of a God who wasn't against us, but was for us.

A God who wasn't far away, but close.

Looking back I know what my grandpa taught me: that there is *always* more to the story. That God isn't done. He would glance down at the closed Bible, at the old pages, and he would say:

"That isn't the end of the story--the story isn't done."

Jesus is God's way of saying the story isn't done.

Jesus in your life is God saying that your story isn't done.

That the end, is never *really* the end.

That if you got stuck hearing people talk about a God who is always waiting for you to do better, or be better, or act better--that you've missed the story of God. If you feel like your life is in the middle of nowhere, God meets you there. God meets his people in the wilderness and gives them a future.

That God's story is all about *incarnation*.

That God hasn't forgotten or abandoned his creation. That while we were drowning, God wasn't shouting from the sidelines, "stop drowning, swim better", but actually dove straight in, with his clothes on, to save us.

I understood this, but I still didn't get Jesus. It didn't sound like a very good story.

Because to me the story sort of sounded like this: God messed up big time when he, you know, made the universe because people were all jacked up (which people tried to peg on Adam and Eve but they were kinda just tossed into difficult working conditions), and so he said to his son Jesus, "listen, this is all a mess and I've got a lot on my plate so I'm going to just ship you in for a while, to set some things in order." So he sent Jesus to die (sorry dude) and then Jesus died, and after he died he was all, "psych not dead", and everybody was like, "whoa fooled us", and then they high-fived and God was like "great job!" and that was basically it. And now because of all that stuff, it was super important for me to wear my itchiest collared shirt to this stuffy room where adults in equally

itchy clothes pretended to sing, then listened
to somebody talk.

I didn't get it.

I bet you've had moments where you didn't
get it either.

But what I was missing was that God was for
us all along.

That what God did with Jesus and the cross
and an empty tomb was what he had been
doing for his creation all along: loving us with
everything he had.

Incarnation means God looked at all the
mess, saw it, and did something. Incarnation
is a great story because it's the story of God
coming here.

And that I could have a conversation with this
God was what made it real.
Incarnation means to take on flesh. To
become a part of the whole thing. Like God
writing himself into the story. Jesus isn't some
religious idea. Some far away concept. He's a
person. Who does person stuff. One writer in
scripture describes Jesus as:

"The visible image of the invisible God."

It's easy to think that God isn't close. To see him as something way up in the sky. There's nothing in the Bible about God having a white beard or a robe, or heaven being some cloud resort where you pluck a harp for all of forever in a diaper. Most of that got taken straight out of ancient mythology. God spends a lot of time talking about heaven coming here, right now, and that one day forever will look a lot more like a city than a cloud. If you don't believe that when you die you'll be a chubby baby in the sky lounging around with this guy with a Gandalf beard--if all that sounds like a fairytale to you, don't worry, you're not alone. I think so too.

If you don't believe in a God who hates, or causes people to suffer, or who only likes people who follow all the rules, that's okay. I don't believe in that God either.

What I see people telling stories about in scripture is a God spending most his time talking about helping us forgive, and love others more than we care about ourselves, and ending injustice, and racism, and taking care of the world he gave us, and not cheating on each other, and rescuing people who are lost or stuck, and breaking addictions to all the things that make us feel like garbage, and sucker-punching shame, beating death, and creating a new world along with him.

That's a God I can believe in. I want to be a part of that.

I'm guessing you do too.

For centuries people tried to get to God.

But what happens when God comes here? When God enters into his creation?

A lot of people I know, especially my friends, think God is far away. Or say things like, "why do bad things happen to good people?" or "how could God allow death, or rape, or genocide, or school shootings, or divorce, or innocent kids to get cancer and die, or parents to lose their jobs?"

I get that.

Jesus is God saying he isn't done with his creation.

Jesus is God's way of getting into the mess and not just getting messy but experiencing the mess. There is a story of Jesus where he loses a really good friend and it says that he wept.

Those are really powerful words.

Because God doesn't just see our pain, or grief, or anguish--he wears it. He puts it on, and says, "Yeah this really hurts".

Jesus skips over the religious people and spends his time with hookers, and outcasts, and wanderers, and adventurers, and dropouts, and everybody not picked for the team. Jesus doesn't chose power but takes the road of the cross and suffers so that we can have life and life to the fullest.

And that story, to me, is a great story.

GOOD LUCK AND GOOD NIGHT
FEBRUARY, *JUNIOR YEAR OF HIGH SCHOOL*

My bedroom is clean for the first time in
months. Clean is a relative term, I know. To
clarify: there are no longer balled-up stray
socks in mounds like mold spores, huddled in
the corners of my room. My swivel office chair
isn't a sitting place for *all* of my clothes.
Books, homework, papers, notes, and blue
lined paper with pencil math equations are no
longer the thick layer canvassing my floor. To
even get to that level I had to manage the
computer cords, headphones, game system
cords, and other arbitrary cords that had
interwoven themselves into an entanglement.

My bedroom also smells better.

First, I took two spray air fresheners from
under the bathroom sink and unloaded two full
clips on the room like I was Master Chief. I
meticulously sprayed the ceiling, walls, desk
drawers--soaking everything in them, and
even went as far as spraying under my
mattress, where I also found a rather awkward
school picture of an ex-girlfriend from seventh
grade, next to a five-dollar bill and a mix-tape

burned on a CD labeled "PARTY!" in Sharpie. I wondered if these three items had anything to do with the other, or if they were a strange, long-forgotten remnant of junior high. The five dollars was a win, and I was especially glad to rid my room of any picture of junior high girls with a face full of braces and blue eyeshadow. I put the disc into my computer and let all the emotion of junior high spill over me. The mixtape, as with the chemical stability of a junior higher's brain, had no middle ground--it was either incredibly cheerful or it was manically angry and depressing.

After the air freshener cans were empty, I poured fabric softener in a bowl, mixed in two parts water, and a fancy shampoo my mom uses, and rubbed it into the carpet. This technique, unknown to most teenagers, is really my secret sauce when cleaning my room. The trick is to not use too much on the floor, but just enough to fluff and scent the carpet. You will experience a soft you have never in your life experienced. If it is an emergency, let's say you left a bowl of chili and your workout spandex shorts under a wet towel for all of summer, you can substitute in baby shampoo and squeeze in fresh lemon. My room hasn't been this clean since the start of school. I cleaned it before the first day because I needed to find a summer book report I had done back in June somewhere in my room. Junior Year felt strange from the beginning. From that first day. It felt darker. Less colorful. We'd had a cold, rainy summer, so by the time school started it never felt like a summer break. Grabbing the latch to my locker that first day back felt wrong. It's that feeling you get when first thing in the morning you spill scalding hot coffee on yourself, or "reply all" on an embarrassing email, or trip getting out of the shower and tangle yourself up in the curtain--it's the feeling that you've begun some domino effect of doom in the universe where everything can only get worse.

Also, that first day of school I wore slippers.

The first day of school is for new school clothes and excited faces, and lingering tans, and an unsaid rule that this is the new, best version of you ever.

Not a pair of slippers.

It wasn't that my family couldn't afford new shoes--I had deliberately made the decision to wear my slippers. It was like every bone in my body was defiant of this school year. I couldn't accept that summer was over. Junior year felt like the last half hour of a really long movie where everybody had forgotten what the movie was about or why we were watching it. My whole junior class looked bored. We all sounded worn out already and it was the first day of school. Girls who normally did the full make-up and outfit routines were in sweats and rain jackets. We observed the wide-eyed underclassmen still obsessing over the whole new school year charade and popularity hierarchy.

I felt like the junior class as a whole was just done. Whatever it was that had given us our motivation these last few years was fully drained.

Here I was, smack dab in the middle of the school year with nothing really to show for it. I stood in awe of the organized room. My room is a matchbox, rectangle-shaped room in the basement I was given permission to inhabit and move into my freshman year. My childhood room was on the main floor of the house beside my sister's and across from the living room. There is no upstairs, just a main floor and basement. The basement is huge, divided into a den, spare bedroom, bathroom, and an unfinished storage we call "the shop" that I think every family has whether it's a garage or attic. It's the place where boxes stack and collect dust and every kid is pretty sure is haunted. The shop is full of old sports equipment, loose screwdrivers, boxes from my parents' childhoods, cobwebs, Christmas decorations, a dusty piano that was my grandma's, garden tools, all the stuff from growing up my mom has to keep 'cause she's my mom but no longer has any place for: stuffed animals in plastic tubs, Star Wars action figures, pictures drawn with crayons, photographs taken of smaller versions of my sister and I on vacations.

It took some convincing for me to get the room I have. I am the only tenant living in one of my parents' downstairs units. I had to build trust. It's basically my own apartment. Okay, not quite, but it's away from everybody and has its own exit and entrance. Christen, my sister, is perfectly content with her childhood room. My old room has been converted to my dad's office. He has a network IT job so there are desks topped with computers and cables and routers and hard drives.

I painted the long sidewalls of my new room Tar Heels blueish-grey and the very back short wall a deep Oxford blue. I pinned up surf posters. There's a framed pencil drawing of Clint Eastwood from The Good, the Bad, and the Ugly I got from a garage sale. The Clash's iconic London Calling poster is above my desk. I have a record player on the far end of the room that I got for Christmas this year.

I built a high rise to put my bed on out of 4x8s. It takes up about half the room and looks more like a stage or a platform than a typical

bed frame. I painted it white. My bed is in the middle, but the whole thing is big enough for me to stand on either side of the bed. There's a hammock hanging in a corner by the closet. It's actually a hammock chair I got in Tijuana, Mexico on a family vacation. The vacation wasn't to Tijuana--it was to San Diego, and we drove through the border for an afternoon culture lesson. And to get knock-off sunglasses. Mostly, I remember it as the trip where I got to drink all the soda I wanted because the water wasn't drinkable, and that a man in a market tried to bargain his jewelry for my then-thirteen-year-old sister for his son's hand in marriage. I pulled my parents aside and quietly, so my sister couldn't hear, said, "I know it sounds crazy, but maybe we should take him up on it. Hear me out, maybe she'd be happy here."
Neither of them thought it was funny.

I cleaned my room cause Anna came over for a while that Friday afternoon after the show. We were both exhausted the next day at school. I hadn't gotten home until three in the morning after dropping her off. I'd thought about kissing her at the door of her house but we were both half asleep and I was pretty sure it wasn't the right moment. After school I said she should stop by and we could hang out. She sat in the hammock for a while kicking against the wall and spinning slowly while I played the junior high mix-tape I'd found and we laughed about the pop songs we secretly still loved.

Finally it got quiet with neither of us saying anything. We were both exhausted. Neither knew what to talk about. It was quiet for a while. I wondered if whatever we had felt the night before had slipped away while we were asleep. I wondered if it was gone. The thought made me sad but I was too tired to be sad. She said she should go and get home. I nodded and said that was probably a good idea. She left and I felt angst. I wanted confirmation of our relationship. Was I in danger of being "friend zoned" like some sort of endless relationship killer quarantine where I'd get stuck being the nice guy and her and her new boyfriend would come over in HAZMAT suits and visit me and I'd make them dinner and cry alone later? I cringed at the thought. It made me sick to my stomach--the way you feel sick when you look at your phone for too long in the car. A sort of gnawing, sour feeling. Whatever this was that we were doing, I needed to know whether she had feelings for me, too.

Lying in my bed that night I wondered about the night before.

Brain:
Remember last night when you were thinking
about whether you loved her?

Me:
Yeah.

Brain:
Let's talk about that.

Me:
What?

Brain:
You know what! Don't what me.

Me:
What do you mean?

Brain:
I mean--no you don't. I mean seriously dude?
I mean--you just met her.

Me:
No I didn't.

Brain:
But you just started talking.

Me:
People fall in love. They go to concerts and
they fall in love. That's a thing. That's life.
That's the way it works. You're trying to stop
me from finding something good. You've tried
to sabotage me all year. Any time anything
good happens you step in and shut it down. I
overthink everything because of you.

Brain:
You're losing control of yourself. You are
falling apart. You're lying to yourself. Pull
yourself together.

Me:
That's not true. I'm in control. Did you see the
way I gave her the tickets? How cool was
that?

Brain:
You are not some hero.

Me:
I didn't say I was.

Brain:
This isn't love. It isn't even infatuation. She
could be anyone. Anywhere. You just want to
feel like somebody likes you. You just don't
want to feel so alone. It's not about her. It's all
about you. Listen to me! It's all about you, not
her. Don't bring her into your mess. You want

to be the hero. You want to be the guy who
swoops in. She just showed up at your
doorstep and could be anyone.

Me:
That's not true.

Brain:
Think about it, you have this awesome year
and then you get to your junior year and you
actually have to act like an adult, your grades
count, and your reputation, and your friends
are all busy. You have all this suppressed
frustration and boredom and stress and worry
and the first girl who pops up you think you
"love" her. Your word for love is really just a
cover for some really deep stuff.

Me:
I'm not worried. What would I have to be
worried about?

Brain:
Do you really want me to tell you?

Me:
Go ahead.

Brain:
Seriously?

Me:
Sure.

Brain:
In no particular order: getting into college, taking the SAT, retaking the SAT after you do poorly, your grades in school, how guilty you feel about not playing basketball this year because you know how much it meant to your mom and dad, your relationship with your parents, the amount you lie about little stuff and worry if you'll be found out, wondering what people who know you think of you, wondering about what people who don't know you think about you, wondering about a girlfriend you'll one day have, analyzing minor flaws in your personality that could potentially be enough for no girl to ever want to marry you, questioning your own sanity, wondering if you are a psychopath and won't find out until much later in life, wondering if you are doing things right now you will regret later in life, wondering if you are a future horrible person and you have no idea now but could have done something to change that, why you haven't been sleeping, why when you sometimes eat cheese you get diarrhea, what's that bump on your thigh that won't go away, could it be cancer, do you have cancer, how can you find out if you have cancer without going to a doctor and having to ask if you have cancer, who will you vote for when

you can vote, you should call your grandma, how much longer will your grandparents really be alive, what if they die, what if you die, what happens in the last few seconds before you die, what if you are afraid, what if you are lonely, what if you die all by yourself, what if you die without doing things you wanted to do, what if you drown, what if you choke, what if you get shot by a stray bullet, what if you are killed in a freak accident, what if you are killed by a friend, what if you have no friends, what if your whole life is a show on TV and you don't know it, what if nobody likes you and they are all pretending, what if you don't amount to anything, what if you're a disappointment, what if everybody finds out who you really are, what if your life is a lie, what if your faith is a joke...keep going.

Me:
I get it...you can stop.

Brain:
Are you sure? I can do this all day.

Me:
Do you just store all this up there?

Brain:
It has to go somewhere. You don't do anything with it so it's my job to keep it. Maybe if you had some kind of healthy outlet.

Me:
Like what?

Brain:
I don't know. A therapist? I'm not the right
person. Don't forget, I'm you.
Me:
I just try and go with the flow.

Brain:
You don't go with the flow--you want to be in
charge of the flow. Your version of go with the
flow is stuffing it all in for me to carry around.

Me:
I can't deal with this. I had a great night and
now you're messing it all up.

Brain:
All I am saying is "love" isn't the right word.

Me:
Then what's the right word?

Brain:
Delusion maybe? *Fantasy*? *Misinterpretation*?

Me:
How about I actually am in love, and you're
wrong, not me?

Brain:
But that's not the case. That's insane. You'd
tell you that. Somewhere deep down you
know, that you know, that you know.
Me:
You can't prove that it's not love I'm feeling.

Brain:
It's not. Trust me. Your word "love" is all
jacked up, my friend.

Me:
I am going to go to sleep and when I wake up
I am going to go over to her house and talk
this whole thing out.

Brain:
You're just pushing it all on me. I have to deal
with your emotional neglect.

Me:
We used to be friends, we used to like each
other.

Brain:
You use me. You don't actually want to be
friends.

Me:
Yes, I do.

Brain:
No, you don't--if you did you wouldn't leave me with all this crap to clean up. You stuff all your baggage on me. You expect me to just take care of all of it. That's not a friendship. You're using me.

Me:
You just want to control me.

Brain:
I want you to realize what's going on before it all crashes down on you. My job is to protect you. That's what I've done your whole life. I'm here for you.

Me:
I can do this on my own!

Brain:
No you can't!

Me:
You don't believe in me.

Brain:
YOU ARE SO DYSFUNCTIONAL! This is your brain and I'm the voice of reason and I'm telling you that you are full of so much pent-up shame and stress and broken expectations that you are in no place to be in a relationship.

It's like unstable nitroglycerine in here. It's not *if* it blows up, but good friend, it's *when*.

Me:
I'll prove you wrong, watch.

Brain:
If you had *my* job, if you had to work in this environment, with all the stuff you've got going on in here--you wouldn't be saying that.

CHOKING HAZARD
TEN YEARS AFTER JUNIOR YEAR OF HIGH SCHOOL

When I was born I almost died.

The umbilical cord was wrapped around my soft little neck seven times. The more I struggled, kicked, and fought, the more tangled I became. I don't remember any of it, *obviously*--but I know some doctor had to slice open my mom's abdomen and snatch my blue, limp self out like some half dead alien. I've always been proud of baby me, for a couple of reasons. First, after my horrific battle against death, which I fought heroically, I immediately urinated on the nurse. I actually don't know why exactly I am proud of this particular moment, I am usually heavily opposed to anybody urinating on strangers, especially those who just saved your life--but there is something so epic about me battling for hours against an umbilical cord strangling me like a python and then peeing on a complete stranger.

I also have always been proud of myself for not dying.

Not dying is a big win. I don't think we give each other enough credit on a day-to-day basis for simply not dying. I mean if you think about it, you've spent a majority of your life not dying. Good for you. Celebrate that. You had a crappy day? Got fired? Failed that test? Tried to eat a burrito while driving and ended up with hot ground beef on your crotch? But *did you die*? Nope. Good for you. Yay you!

There I was, all six pounds of me, tangled up and gasping for life.

Sometimes I wonder if deep down, inside my subconscious, I know the terror of that moment. Maybe it's why lots of nights I have some form of nightmare that I can never totally remember, but wake up sweaty, yelling and upside down in bed, or aimlessly sleepwalking through the halls of my house half-awake.

I do know that almost dying in that moment, it shows me something about our human struggle.

See, that umbilical cord, which was my source of life, which fed me nutrients and supplied me with all the things I needed, ended up straight up turning on me and strangling me.

There are all these things that end up wrapping around us and suck the life out of us even though we think they are helping us.

For me, it was religion. It was feeling like I needed to follow all the rules just right. To be perfect. Or pretend to be perfect. To know all the right answers.

It smothered me. Suffocated all the life inside me.

———————

At the end of fifth grade my mom told me she got a job at a private school as a P.E. teacher, this gave her free tuition, which she passed off to my sister and I. It's why I got to go to the school I did. I didn't choose it. I love my mom and I think she honestly wanted the best for me by sending me there. She worked really hard so I could have a great education.

I remember the day when she came home and told us she'd got the job. I would start my sixth grade at a private school with all new friends. It was a kindergarten through twelfth grade school. All in one. Can you imagine this for a second? There were like seventeen year olds in the same building as children who still kept an extra pair of pants in their classrooms in case of an emergency bowel movement. The school tried to be intentional with where every age group was located but occasionally you passed a first grader on your way to physics. It was like some jacked up physiological stuff.

Going in, I knew nobody.

Except Blake.

Blake enrolled a month before school started.

Blake and I were in the same preschool. We met on the playground. Since then we've been friends.

At private school we made a pact. A bond of sorts. We'd make it through together. We have each other's backs. There was this assignment we had the first week of school--it was a dream-board the teacher said--where we had to answer questions about who we wanted to be when we graduated. One question said, "what is your biggest and best goal for when you graduate?"

Which is freakin' absurd to ask a sixth grader to make that mental leap. Like they can't even comprehend the end of the school year--but anyway we were imagining our lives six years into the future. And Blake wrote, "be best friends with Bryan" and I wrote, "be best friends with Blake". Like that was our one goal. That was the agreement. Ride this thing out.

Best friends.

Sixth grade was survival. Then came seventh grade. Everything in seventh grade revolved around popularity. We stood our ground together. Started skateboarding. Argued over best bands of all time. Managed to kiss a girl on the bus on the way back from a basketball game. Bombed math tests. Aced advanced English. At one point in time we thought it'd be cool to get the same shoes, pants, and sweatshirt--so in an incredibly strange, and mildly embarrassing moment, we wore the same clothes for a season at school as awkward preteens.

I can't speak for all private schools, there must be some really great ones who practice the stuff they preach--ours didn't. It was pretending to be perfect. It was judging others. We were expected to behave. To act a certain way. To color inside the lines. It all felt fake. I felt fake. I felt like I was learning how to be a Pharisee.

If you don't know who the Pharisees are, they were the religious leaders in Jesus' day. The Pharisees spent most of their time trying to protect God's holiness. They decided who was in and who was out. They were supposed to help people experience God, but instead most of the time they judged people.

It's the Pharisees who plot how to straight up murder Jesus. Think of the irony here, the person who has the power to save them, who is the literal walking-and-talking version of the God they worship, and they miss it. Not only that, they are against it.

You can get so caught up in religion that you miss Jesus.

You can get so caught up in your own thing that you are against God's thing without realizing it.

That's pretty scary.

Don't get me wrong, there were some great teachers and people at that school and I don't want to say everybody was terrible and I was awesome. Hear me out--I was watching myself become a hypocrite. I saw it in myself. I began to realize I was living in this Christian bubble. That school gave me a context for how easy it is to fall into the trap of hypocrisy. Where the church cares more about what they are against than what they are for. It showed me how easy it is to forget your purpose.

Jesus says to the religious leaders that they are like a tomb that's white washed on the outside while everything inside is dead. Jesus says his kingdom is the opposite of that.

In Jesus' day, the Pharisees represented who God was to people. And people felt like they weren't good enough. I remember in high school not feeling good enough at that school a lot.

What do you do when you don't feel good enough? You either conform or lash out. I lashed out.

In ninth grade my friend Tyler and I were supposed to decorate the hallways. I don't know why. I don't remember anyone else ever decorating our school halls. We had to choose a theme and then use crate paper to add life to the school's halls. We were all over it. We chose an 'under the sea' theme--including large colorful paper cutouts of ocean waves, seaweed and lots of fish. I mean it was a freakin' aquarium of fish. Like up and down the lockers, lining the classroom doors, and waving hi to you as you walked into school. We glued, taped, and constructed an epic underwater adventure. Okay, *okay*--yes, it wasn't just because we were thrilled with under the sea life--mostly it was because all of our fish looked like one particular male body part poorly disguised as jumping fish. Our glorious ninth grade humor masterpiece lived a full day of school, with oblivious teachers, and hundreds of students saying hi to our aquatic friends.

Remember: my mom worked at the school. She took one glance down the hallway and was like, "Nope. Shut it down. Those are *not* fish."

I was frustrated with a system that felt suffocating so I lashed out.

The people in Jesus' day were frustrated with the system as well. They felt strangled by religion. They felt beat down. Jesus says to them:

"Come to me, all of you who are weary and carry heavy burdens, and I will give you rest."

We are all broken people who need a rescuer. Because that's the gospel. That's the good news that Jesus says is so good it's worth dying for.

There's a moment where Jesus looks at his disciples and asks them who they think he is. The one who answers says he is the Messiah. The rescuer. The one who's coming to put things right. The one who is going to beat death.

You are messy. You are broken. But you are more loved than you could ever imagine. You are forgiven. Everything in your life is being made new when you discover Jesus.

The question is: who do you say Jesus is?

I'd hate to get all the head knowledge. Know all the right answers but miss Jesus.

Think about Judas. He's famously the disciple who betrayed Jesus to the religious leaders. He's been with Jesus his whole ministry. Years of walking, talking, listening, learning, thinking, processing, praying, and seeing miracle after miracle. Think about it, he's as close as you can get to Jesus. Jesus picked him for the team. He isn't just in the crowd. He's a part of feeding five thousand people with a loaf of bread and a few fish. He's just inches away from paralyzed people taking their first steps. He's right there when Jesus says he and God are the same person. Judas is with Jesus, next to him, looking at him face to face. Do you ever wish you could just have that kind of relationship with Jesus? Like Judas has Jesus on speed dial. He had him day or night. Ever wish that you could have been there with Jesus? Seen the stuff Jesus did? I do. Honestly, I think that would be helpful.

Judas has that kind of connection with Jesus. He knows all the right answers. He's heard every story. Seen every sign. And still he betrays Jesus. You can be close to Jesus and still miss Jesus. You can grow up in the church and still miss the mission. You can be from a family of faith and still fail to see the future God has for you.

It's why Jesus keeps healing blind people.

It's a miracle
And it's a *metaphor*.

As the song says, *I once was blind but now I see*.

You are a miracle and a metaphor. You are both. You are what God has done and what God *is doing*. You are what God has done and *will do*. You are what God is doing for the whole universe. Blindness to sight. Broken to healing.

There's one story where Jesus spits on some dirt and rubs it on this guy's eyes. After that he can see. He was blind from birth and then he can see. I don't like spit. I don't want people to spit on me. Or near me. Spit's fine when it's in the mouth. But once it's out, I'm out. Spit is gross.

I certainly don't want them spitting on dirt and rubbing it in my eyes.

Jesus doesn't have to do it this way. He could just say a word and the guy would see. He's done it before. So why the saliva and mud, Jesus? Why put this guy through that? I think Jesus is making a point about our blindness. We are spiritually blind. From birth we can't see anything. We are walking in darkness. Lost. Lonely. Empty.

Jesus comes along and knows it's only he who can save us. Do we want Jesus or do we just want the miracle? Do we want all of Jesus? Are we okay stepping out of our comfort zone? Are we okay with a little messiness? Do we want God or do we just want his gifts?

I was strangled by religion.
Maybe there is something else you've felt strangled by.
Jesus meets us in the middle.
The gospel says we are broken and God is all we need.

Shame isn't the thing. Grace is the thing. Love is the thing. Hope is the thing. Jesus isn't just an idea; he's a person.

He's God reaching down, into our mess, and pulling us out of the religion in which we've gotten ourselves tangled up--in all the ways we think we can get to God.

GO TO THE MOVIES,
JUST FOR THE PREVIEWS
TEN YEARS AFTER JUNIOR YEAR OF HIGH SCHOOL

We don't call my grandma, *grandma*; we call her *Gummy*.

I guess the first grandchild to come along was supposed to call her *Grammy* but it all got lost in translation. All I know is that by the time I jumped on the scene it was *Gummy* and instead of *Papa* it was *Pampa*.

Gummy and Pampa.

The first thing you'd notice about her is the smile. It isn't the typical warm, or soft elderly smile, rather it's young and full and mischievous. Like the grin of a teenage girl texting underneath the table during dinner.

Gummy lives in this traditional redbrick New England style home smack dab in the southern California suburbs of Orange County. She wears white Keds, loves French fries, and has a knack for singing Judy Garland era show tunes. She doesn't cook or

120

bake, as she says, "I'm just not that kind of grandma."
Gummy is great at telling stories.

First, because she has a sense of humor and general sense of irony, and second, because she is constantly reading history, biographies, and all sorts of books.

We all have different ways of saying *I love you*.
Gummy's way of saying *I love you* is to tell you a story.

There's this one she tells about soup crackers. Wait--let me back up. Gummy tells the same stories a lot. She'll start and Pampa will chime in with a, "jeez they've heard it already." It's not because she's senile or old, but merely because she's really, freaking good at telling stories. It reminds me of what it must have been like before TV or radio or Netflix. You sit there glued, even though you know what's coming because you love the story. You love the person telling the story.

It's a gift.

So every time we go to this local fish restaurant Gummy will do this bit where she'll pick up her menu for complete show, then look around the table, as if teasing her audience as say, "I'm having the halibut, just for the halibut."

To which she tells the story of the soup crackers.

Basically, the short version is that somebody in the family a long time ago, in a galaxy far, far away, didn't want their little oyster crackers that came with clam chowder. I can't remember who started it, if it was her or whoever the person was, again she tells it better--but at some point somebody hid the crackers in the other person's suitcase when they left and it started this like twenty year game of hiding oyster crackers in suitcases and other strange places.

It's a good story.
We need good stories.
Grace is a good story.

Grace is the story of a God who isn't far away, but close. Grace is God's way of showing that he hasn't given up. Grace is the story of us and God and forever.

But it's one of those kinds of stories, where if you don't tell it right, it totally sucks.

Okay, maybe not *suck*, but you have to tell it right. Grace is a storyteller's teed-up homerun.

Grace is the story of what God is doing in his creation, in you, and in all of everything all along. Since the beginning, grace is this wrecking-ball obliterating shame. Demolishing selfishness. Crushing sin. Setting us free. If it's sin vs. grace--grace wins every time. Hands down. No contest. It's this story that's been playing out since the beginning of time and if you tell it right, there's nothing better.

When I go to the movies, I go for the previews or what they call in the movie industry: the trailers. Those first ten minutes when the theater dims half dark, as if to say, "listen, we're going to start some business here, but we're easing into all of it."

My family knows if we're going to see some new movie, we are getting there early. I sit wide-eyed during the previews. I give commentary, exclaiming, "I can't wait for that" or "that looks amazing" or "that looks like the worst movie."

People have called me a trailer snob.

I am a critic. I am a connoisseur. I am a movie trailer aficionado.

Here's the thing about the previews, they have to tell you a compelling story in less than three minutes and make it meaningful. Their whole job is to give you just enough of the story that you have an emotional response and eventually go see the movie. There is subtlety to this. You can't flat out give me everything, but I also have to be sucked in. When it's done right--it's incredible.

You are left wanting more.
You are left with a sense of awe.
You are left with curiosity.

Sitting there, watching the glaring green "approved for all ages" slide, I can feel myself beginning to have an emotional experience.

It's a great feeling. Questions start swarming. What is coming out next? Who's going to be in it?

For a trailer to work, I mean really work, the music has to be perfect. The chosen scenes have to be compelling. The splices have to have movement.

I have literally teared up during trailers.
Sometimes I feel called to action.
Other times I am inspired.

I'll go back on the Internet and watch them over and over.

Trailers take us somewhere. They are their own art. They take us somewhere new and exciting and confusing and real.

Everything God is doing is a trailer.

I want to say this again, because I don't want you to miss it. Everything God is doing, and has done throughout history, is a trailer. It's a sneak peak at a bigger story. It's a piece to the puzzle. It's a montage of his love for us. It's a small slice of the whole picture. Grace is God's trailer for a life with him forever. Grace says the best is yet to come. The cross is God's trailer for the forgiveness of sin. The resurrection is the trailer for what will happen to those of us in Christ when we die. It's a good story that's leading into a great story. It's a reminder that there is more to come. Grace leads us further into the mystery of God's love and the future he has for us. Grace is God desiring to have us as his kids. Everything you have is a gift from a Father who loves you.

It's all a gift.

There's a woman in the story of Jesus who comes face-to-face with grace. Jesus is teaching as he usually did. Pointing out what God had done in the past and what he was going to do in the future. Jesus was always teaching this idea that heaven was something that could intersect with the ordinary. The kingdom of heaven was kicking off now. Jesus is teaching and he gets interrupted. The religious leaders sprawl this woman in front of Jesus. She's just been caught cheating. Now, obviously adultery is not good. Nobody would say cheating on somebody is the right thing to do. It's ugly, and hurtful, and selfish--if you've ever been cheated on you know what it feels like. You know why God says that we shouldn't sleep around on our husband or wife or girlfriend or boyfriend or whoever. This woman is in the wrong. She broke the laws that God had given to the Israelites.

This girl she gives herself up to somebody else. She breaks what she had with this other person. The person she says she loves, she sneaks behind their back to be with somebody else. She gets in bed with a person who is not her husband.

The religious leaders try and trap Jesus. They want something they can use against him. If he says "it's no big deal", he is dismissing her sin and letting her off the hook. If he says "yeah let's kill her right here and now", well that surely doesn't sound like the message he's preaching.
Maybe you know the thing that would most embarrass you if people found out.

How often do we just wear masks and feel like, if anybody knew the real us, we'd be destroyed. This is the girl's worst nightmare.

I also want you to notice something else about this story, which I love.

In the ancient Near East in Jesus' day, women had zero rights. They were property. They were objects. They were powerless. You and I know that's not okay. That even today in our world we see way too much exploitation, degradation, intolerance, and straight up sexism towards women. Back then it was worse. Anybody who tries to use the Bible to defend the mistreatment of women has missed Jesus. He don't play that game. Watch him in the gospels. He's always sticking up for the underdogs. It's as if he sees everybody as created by God. As if all colors, backgrounds, nationalities, and personalities are a part of God's family. Jesus steps up. In front of this boys' club of religious leaders, Jesus shrugs and steps in front of the moving train. Jesus is the type of guy who sticks up for girls who just got caught cheating.

They have all picked up rocks. In their culture the price you paid for this sin was death by rock throwing. You just stood there and people chucked rocks at you until you were dead. Pretty brutal.

Grace doesn't let you off the leash.
It doesn't overlook sin.
It looks it dead in the eyes.

Standing there Jesus does something
unexpected. He looks around at all these
people standing there ready to kill this girl. He
looks at them, beside her.

"All right," Jesus says, his words meeting each
person exactly where they are, "but let the one
who has never sinned throw the first stone!"

Grace is a mic drop.
Jesus says, "Never sinned? Have at it."
Jesus says, "Lived a perfect life? Go ahead."

It's as if he's saying that we are all broken and
we all need to ask for forgiveness. It's as if the
only thing we have to brag about is our faith in
him.

One writer of the Bible says:

"If you want to boast, boast only about the
Lord."

We have all been caught cheating on God.
We all have broken the heart of our Creator.
We have all messed up.

It says in the story that all these religious leaders, they leave oldest to youngest. There is something about the older you get the more you know how imperfect you are. I love imagining these old dudes putting down these rocks they were going to use to kill her. You can hear the thud of rocks hitting the ground.

Then it's just Jesus and her. Standing at the scene of the crime. She's shaking. Terrified. Tears racing down her cheeks. She didn't deserve this. She deserved to die. She knew what she was getting into. She's not dumb. But she's standing there with her savior.

When you stand with your savior and you look death in the face, stuff inside you changes. The story says:
 "Then Jesus stood up again and said to the woman, 'Where are your accusers? Didn't even one of them condemn you?'"

"'No, Lord,' she said.

"And Jesus said, 'Neither do I. Go and sin no more.'"

Grace is unexpected and undeserved. It's a gift. If you haven't had a face-to-face interaction with grace, stop reading this book. Put it down. Look at the things around you and pray these words:

God, I don't deserve any of this
Thank you
I'm broken
I need you
Help me realize the power of the gospel
And what it's doing all around me.

This is a powerful prayer because God's
grace is not something you get, it's something
you begin to see. His grace doesn't happen
because you changed your life, you change
your life because grace happens. By itself sin
can look really big, beside grace sin gets
really small.

You say I could never stop sinning. That's
impossible.
See what standing side by side with your
savior does to that.
Give Jesus a challenge and see what he
does.

What God does on Easter with an empty
tomb, is merely the trailer for what's coming.
It's a preview. It's a sneak peak.

It's taken me a long time to get here.
The story of Grace isn't about what we've
done or how good we can be.

It's the story of Jesus. The cross was the place where God said this is how far I will go to be with you. Forever.

Jesus is standing beside you.

We all have different ways of saying *I love you.*

"And neither do I condemn you" is Jesus saying *I love you.*

"Go and sin no more" is Jesus saying you are free.

THE PROBLEM WITH GOLF CLUBS
FEBRUARY, *JUNIOR YEAR OF HIGH SCHOOL*

I sleep over at Tyler's house the night before the dance. The dance is on a Saturday so Friday night we prepare mentally the way anybody else would--by eating cheap frozen pizza and lighting fireworks we find in the garage from the Fourth of July eight months ago.

At some point Tyler decides to call his girlfriend and talk for a solid hour while I play Mario Kart quietly in the corner. The music is turned up so loud on his computer I'm surprised he can hear her talking. I am also relieved because I don't have to listen to their pet names for each other and the voice he puts on when she calls. It annoys me. It sounds soft, and pathetic, and creepy.

Tyler and I are friends the way bank robbers are probably friends. You share strategies, benefit mutually, join enterprises but at the end of the day you're not sure who's screwing who over. Tyler is also crazy. I don't mean like, monkeys around a little crazy, I mean I once saw him throw tennis balls out of his car in traffic at innocent drivers with their windows down. He nailed a guy in the head who looked like a mafia thug.

Another time Blake and Tyler and I were at our friend Max's parent's beach cabin and Blake shot Tyler with a Rubber band from across the room so Tyler put Blake's head through a window. The craziest part was Tyler wasn't even mad, he was laughing, as if he'd shot Blake back with the another rubber band. Instead there was glass everywhere and Blake looked disoriented and bloody.

This is the level of crazy. One minute he'd be having a normal conversation and the next he'd be shooting an airsoft gun at your dad.

Tyler would go from the crazed maniac war cry to phone cuddling with his girlfriend and you can see why it weirded me out. I wanted to be like, "you know this guy was trying to light his own hair on fire literally five seconds before whispering I love you."

We are supposed to double date to Tolo-- which part of me is looking forward to because if it gets awkward with Anna, we can always discreetly make fun of Tyler and his girlfriend and wait for Tyler to do something crazy like trip a cop, or dive into an electrical fence, or

steal a golf cart (all of which have happened at least once, if not several times).
The strangest part about Tyler is the girls at our school love him. Not just the girls who are crazy themselves or have daddy issues, but like attractive girls grades older than us who are stable, and pretty, and have jobs at gyms. Actually, girls at other schools love him too. They all think he's handsome, and funny. Sometimes they say he's sweet and I want to throw up a little. I remember one time in class there was a new girl who showed up in the middle of the school year. That afternoon I saw Tyler kissing her in the parking lot as he was getting into his mom's minivan. This was like ninth grade. His mom was in the car and he just kissed the new girl on her first day. His mom waved at her as they drove off.

That doesn't happen.
It was legendary.
People talked about it for weeks.

Another time, on a field trip he was sitting by this girl named Beth who was in love with him. She'd talk about him all the time. Was always trying to conveniently find her way next to him in class. He took one of this girl's shoes off her feet on the bus and threw her size seven Nike out of the window on the highway. It bounced a couple of times and landed smack dab in the middle of a lane. This girl was walking around the Pacific Northwest history museum all lopsided with one shoe on talking about how Tyler was the love of her life. I was like, "this dude just threw your shoe out of a moving vehicle and you're talking about how cute you think he is?!"

It made no sense. We were all baffled. Most the time, when it came to Tyler, we were baffled in one way or another. He also got really good grades. Which was another baffling characteristic to add to the list.

Do you have this friend?

They should be in prison, or Guantanamo Bay, or some kind of program for the insane, yet somehow they get a 4.0. They get tests back in Chemistry with one hundred percent and a smiley face in red ink at the top, while you get a sixty percent and a note that says, "try studying next time." The worst part is you *did* study. For hours. Hours and hours and hours. Time spent memorizing formulas late into the night instead of having any ounce of a social life or hobby. You sacrificed and labored for that sixty percent.

Tyler didn't study. Tyler was busy giving himself a homemade tattoo with a razor, a sowing needle, some duct-tape and a ballpoint pen. Tyler was busy recording a rap

mixtape. Tyler shaved his legs. Tyler shot a how-to-make-napalm video and posted it on the Internet. Tyler disguised himself as an elderly person and spent the night in an old folks home playing cribbage for those innocent elderly's medication. Tyler was exercising jujitsu on unsuspecting Starbuck's baristas. He was rollerblading through the grocery store aisles. He was ordering super sized drinks at a fast food drive-thru and throwing them back into the window yelling, "HIT THE DECK." He was on a date with college girls with volleyball scholarships who had an internship at Microsoft. He was teaching himself how to play the stock market. He was mowing the shag carpet in his basement for fun. He was starting varsity select soccer games while eating a gas station beef burrito on the field mid game; his coach could care less because every college in the country was offering him scholarships.
I studied.
I tried.
I put in the effort.

Whoever said, "hard work pays off" has never been in high school.
They had never met Tyler.
Our freshman year we both went out for the track team. Tyler only did because he wanted to throw the javelin at our classmates. I did because Tyler did. Tyler was an athlete the

way Romans were athletes. He was like a marble statue of some mythical god killing a lion with bare hands. I had the body type of Woody from Toy Story. My head was too big, my frame skinny and sort of wobbly, my long legs dangling out from my torso.

Our coach took one look at me and threw me in with the hurdlers.

Over the course of that season I did pretty well. I was fast enough and lanky enough to hold my own in each race. I wasn't getting first place, but I wasn't getting last either. My times were getting better and better.

In the final race of the season my coach put Tyler in the hurdles with me. He told me I needed somebody to push me. The first time Tyler even jumped over a hurdle was a few minutes before the gun went off. He looked ridiculous.

But Tyler was a brute force. The crack of the pistol went off, and Tyler launched from his blocks--like the Tasmanian Devil from Bugs Bunny cartoons, he was a whirlwind devastating the path of hurdles.
Tyler got first place.
I got fourth.
This was my relationship with Tyler.

I think Tyler was a lonely person. You can have all the friends in the world, have everybody love you, win at everything and be completely empty. I don't think anybody noticed but me. His parents couldn't tell. I know they put a lot of pressure on him. His dad was a star football player in high school. There was a lot of pressure on Tyler to be everything. The problem with that is nobody can be everything, even if you try, there won't be anything left of yourself because you'll be spread so thin.

I feel like a lot of us walk around pretending like we're happy, but there isn't anything left.

We're spread too thin.
We've lost something.
Some vital part of us is missing.

I am not sure Tyler knew how lonely he really was, except for the rare moments when he would let himself admit how he was doing deep down. Even then it was like the pain was buried. Those moments were uncommon. I don't think his girlfriend Emily knew. She was not just one of the most popular girls at our school--she had been the most popular for the longest period of time. Other girls had fought for the top place in our school only to fall to the wayside. Emily had started climbing the ladder of coolness in seventh grade. She was the first to create a 'cool' table in the lunchroom and dominate it. She was pretty but not too pretty, she could be totally cruel yet was kind most of the time, outgoing but quiet when she needed to be. Emily had longevity in the popularity game. It's easy to come up one year and be at the top, but it's just as easy to fall off the map the next year. Popularity is a game you're always playing. You can't turn it off. Once you have it, you always need more of it. She didn't run the school but she was savvy enough to have the most influence.

In high school, influence is everything.

Tyler and her began dating last summer after they had made out by a bonfire on a beach.

Here's what I think: I think it can be just as lonely at the top as you it can be at the bottom. I think you can have everything and have nothing. You can win every time and still lose.

Jesus says you can gain everything in the world and still lose your soul.

He asks, is there anything more important than your soul?

You are not just a body. You are not just
atoms stacked on top of each other. You are
not just a combination of energy, and
molecules, and skin, and bones.
You are not a body that has a soul. You are a
soul, and you have a body.

You are not random.

There is something inside you that is endless.
And Jesus says that's what we should be
thinking about. Not just will we go to heaven--
but what kind of state is our soul in? Too often
we exchange who we are for something that
doesn't matter. Your soul is like a balloon, it
can be inflated--full of hope, and joy, and
wonder, and courage--or it can be deflated,
absent of all those things that it should be full
of.

How is your soul?
Is it inflated?
Or deflated?

"If you try and hang onto your life," Jesus
says, "you'll lose it. But if you give up your life
for my sake and the sake of the Good News,
you'll save it."
It's a powerful thing when you can look over
your life and say, "I'm tired of trying to do this
on my own. I'm sick of fighting for the top. I'm

done exchanging who I am for things that don't matter."

Jesus also says you will have to take up your cross.

It's another way of saying you are going to have to give up your whole life. You are going to have to sacrifice everything. Would you be willing to sacrifice everything to follow Jesus? You will have to sacrifice your coolness, your comfort, and your whole self.

After Tyler gets off the phone he tells me that he's in love. I take him seriously because I've never heard him talk like that. He says she's the one.
Tyler says we should go sit on his porch while he tries to duct-tape sparklers together to make a sparkler bomb, which is what happens when you take a ton of sparklers and duct-tape them together.

The night is crisp with late February frost. Everything looks damp. You can see your breath as pale clouds float away from your face. Somewhere past his lawn and neighbor's swing-set, cars buzz along a busy road.
There's a smell of wet leaves and pine needles and burnt freezer pizza left over from earlier.

"Did I tell you about the dog across the street?" Tyler asks, stretching the tape tight around a handful of metallic sparklers.

"No," I say, staring at a trampoline and wondering why we've never jumped on it. "Maybe, I don't know."

We sit on the stairs of the porch. The ground is wet, the wood of the three steps drenched in rainwater, neither of us seem to care. Tyler's parents aren't home. I don't know where they are. They seem to float in and out without much notice from anybody.

"The house across the street used to have a dog."

"Oh," I say pausing. "Why have we never jumped on your trampoline?"

"Because it's not ours," he says, "it's the other neighbors, the wind picked it up and blew it through all those bushes and over into our lawn, but they yell at us if we get on it."

"Lame."
"Yeah it's bogus. Anyway, not those neighbors, *those* over there," he points across the side of the yard, "used to have this little dog. It was one of those yappy dogs, the kind that get all worked up and chomp their little

mouths and yip at everything. I don't remember its name. I haven't told anybody about this." His tone changes and he looks right at me as though he were deciding whether I am the right person to tell, "One night my parents were out of town. They were gone somewhere. Nobody was home. I still don't know why I did it Bry."

Tyler was one of the few people who call me Bry.

I can't tell if he's going to cry or if it's the icy winter air causing his eyes to look bloodshot and wet. His hands are tight around the tape as he wraps the tiny metal stems. I want to jump on the trampoline. I keep thinking about it but I know it's not the right time. Even from here I can see a thin layer of ice. I picture myself leaping up and landing on my back, shattering the ice into a million pieces.

"But I went to the garage and found my dad's golf clubs. They are these custom clubs he had made for him. I took the nine-iron out. I swear this dog had barked all day and all night. I wasn't mad though. That was the weird part. I wasn't mad. I wasn't angry. I was focused. It was a night like this. It was cold. I walked over to the yard and grabbed the dog." He made a swooping motion with his hands, "I

picked the dog up and it just kept barking.
This little yappy dog, I held it in my jacket."

I start to laugh at the thought of Tyler with a
golf club and a little dog in his jacket, but I
look over and Tyler isn't laughing with me.
Tyler's eyes look hollow. He looks like he
might puke.

All the toughness I had inside me when I was
usually with Tyler was leaking out. I became
scared. Not afraid, but scared. Deeply scared.
The way you're scared when you sense
something evil. Something dark. Not
frightened but disturbed. Tyler's voice
sounded collected but beneath that there was
remorse.

"I brought the dog over by the woods over
there and I hit it with the golf club. I didn't hit it
hard at first. I hit it once and then I just kept
hitting it."

I sat motionless. I realized I was gripping my
fingernails into the splinters of the step beside
me. Everything inside me felt gross. I felt sick.
I was horrified. I couldn't show it. I swallowed
hard.

"I buried it out in the bushes."

I couldn't look at him.

"I just remember the sound of the barking, when it finally stopped."

My stomach turned over.

I didn't know what to say. What do you say? I moved my eyes over to the edge of the woods, the Pacific Northwest evergreen trees casting ominous shadows on the grass of his yard. I imagined Tyler walking this dog over to the woods with the gold club in his hands. I imagined the silence after the barking stopped. I wanted to get up and go home. What causes a person to do such a horrible thing?

"That's really messed up," I said, "like really, *really* messed up."

"Nobody ever found out," he said. "I was in the kitchen and the neighbors, they came to the door and asked my mom if they had seen the dog. They said it was missing. They hung posters around the neighborhood on telephone poles and stuff."

His voice trailed off.
I believe there is evil in this world.

In the very first book of the Bible we see where it all goes down. God creates people, people choose their own way over God's and this ripple effect begins spanning out. We are born into sin.

There is evil. We live in a wounded world. One writer in the Bible says, "Creation looks forward to the day when it will join God's children in glorious freedom from death and decay." They go on to say that the universe is longing to be rescued from the here and now, it's crying out like a women giving birth.

You live long enough you come up against real evil. Things where you look and you say, "That's what sin looks like." Things that you know are wrong. Things that you know are not the way this world was meant to be. Things deep down you know are pretty messed up. I think it's hard to look at the misuse of power and not see clear evil. It's hard to see the mistreatment of children and see evil. You can't watch the news and think, *that's not right.*

Sin is a word people don't like to hear in our culture. I think because we think of people standing on the corners of streets screaming that sinners are going to hell. We think of people saying that dancing is a sin. That sin is just another word people use to control other people. Except, I think there really is a thing called *sin*. I think it weaves its way into us and we can see it in other people but can't see it in ourselves. I think that there is evil in this world.

People always ask why God doesn't just erase all the evil in this world. Why God doesn't just do something. Let's pretend that God could flick a switch and all the evil would just be gone. God finishes His expense reports, grabs another cup of coffee, straightens His tie and flips the old "erase all the evil in the world" switch before heading to lunch. Problem is he's going to have to get rid of you too. Because of all the evil you got stuffed inside you. See, there's all this sin that's found its home in us.

The prophet Isaiah in the Bible says:

"We are all infected and impure with sin." Sin has infected us. It's a cancer that's growing inside.

The problem with sin is nothing helps. Everything feels like Advil. It helps for a little while and then we are back to square one. Everything we do is just another cover-up.

Sin is the symptom of a heart that won't worship God. You can go to church, follow all the rules, never drop a F bomb and still be soaked in sin. Jesus seemed to think that we all need a savior from the sin we are entangled in.

Paul says in his letter to the Romans:

"For everyone has sinned; we all fall short of God's glorious standard."

And then he says,

"Yet God freely and graciously declares that we are righteous. He did this through Christ Jesus when he freed us from the penalty for our sins. For God presented Jesus as the sacrifice for sin."

God's a surgeon. He's patient. He's careful. He's precise. He sees the sin in us and knows this will be a process. It starts with knowing he took the punishment when he walked the road of the cross.

Sitting there on the pavement I felt like I was going to throw up. Tyler had finished and was arranging a single sparkler at the top for a fuse. I'd watched him do it before. It smells like it is going to start raining. He asks me to hold the bottom of the bundle. I reach and grab the cold metal. I watch my breath leave my lungs.
Neither of us say anything.

I don't know what to say. What would you say if your friend told you he beat a neighbor's dog to death? Sin always tells us lies that we are alone. That we have to carry our secrets. That nobody will understand. Or love you. But that's not true. The Bible calls it going into the light. That sin tries to keep us in the darkness--but light, light is freedom. Light is where everything is visible and no longer has any power.

You were created to live in the light.

Was he looking for confirmation? Did he need me to validate that it was wrong? Did he want to hear that it was the right thing to do even though he had to know I thought it was a terrible act of violence against a completely innocent creature? I didn't know how to be a good friend. Or a friend at all. I kind of wanted to hate him in this moment.

"Don't say anything about that," he says. "Nobody else knows."

Is this his confession? Is he bragging?

Or is there another option? Tyler, I think is like the rest of us: we don't know what to do with the horrible things we've done, so we stuff it in and pretend like it didn't happen. I've never committed something like this, but I know I've broken God's heart with my own sin. Tyler killing this dog (as horribly sad and disgusting as this is) is no worse than my sin. Sin is sin. It's inhumane. It makes us less human. It turns us into something we aren't. Jesus came to make us more human. He says he came to bring life and life to the fullest. Sin always leads to death and more death. All sin is horrible and sad and disgusting. It all breaks God's heart.

The Psalmist writes:

"O God, you know how foolish I am; my sins cannot be hidden from you."

We need to name sin. We need to call it out in ourselves. We need to acknowledge how ugly it is. We need to see it in our heart and tell people and ask for forgiveness.

Jesus takes our place for our sin on the cross. That's the beautiful picture of who God is.

Jesus is God's way of saying evil doesn't win.

The cross is God's way of taking sin head on. The resurrection is God's way of defeating death forever.

Jesus, hanging up on the cross says:
"It is finished."

It would have taken everything he had left to say this.
But he wanted you to know. To hear it. To feel it.

You need to know in your soul that Jesus beat sin and death.

I wish I had said more to Tyler. I wish I had told him that we all have fallen short of God's standard. I wish looking back that as Tyler was fiddling for the lighter in his pocket I would have looked him in the eyes and said, "that's horrible what you did--but it doesn't define you."

I think his soul needed to be set free and I missed it.

I wish I had said, "When the power of Christ takes over your life, grace defeats death. You are forgiven. You are made new." Right there sitting on the steps before we got up, I wish I would have said, "I know that isn't who you are. I know you are created for more. I know the rest of your life will look different because you will either think of yourself as a jacked up dog murderer or you will think of yourself as made new by Christ."

I didn't say any of it.

I was too freaked out. Maybe looking back it
made me realize the job I have here on earth
to share the message of who Jesus is. Or
maybe, Tyler just needed a friend who would
sit with him and love him. Maybe sometimes
we don't realize that we share who Jesus is by
not walking away. By just being with
somebody.

Paul says in his letter to the Romans,
"For the wages of sin is death," he says, "but
the free gift of God is eternal life through
Christ Jesus our Lord."

Sin is real.
Sin also isn't the end of the sentence.
Just on the other side is Jesus.

SAY, I'M A BIRD
FEBRUARY, *JUNIOR YEAR OF HIGH SCHOOL*

I'd gone to her house. We'd made dinner: homemade pizza, the kind where you make the dough and toss on all these fancy toppings like mozzarella and sage and chicken. Across from her house there was a small garage turned living room where we sat on a large L-shaped couch and ate. I began to realize that this was a date. It was a few weeks after we'd gone to Tolo and this had all the classic symptoms of a date:

1. Talk of other couples at school and how basically they were dumb, instigating subtly that we were awesome.

2. Scrupulous analyzing of what movie to watch. Nothing says dating like picking out a movie. Non-dating or friend zones are always defined by aimless TV watching, or worse: watching a show one person wants to watch but is halfway through the fourth season and just expects the other person to pick up what's going on. If you're stuck watching season 3 of One Tree Hill because she wants to and you haven't seen season 1-2, you're not dating.

Also, and I'm not kidding at all, she picked The Notebook. Nothing, I mean nothing says, "I'm in" like when a girl says let's watch The Notebook. Just to be clear, dudes if you pick The Notebook she'll probably think you're creepy. She has to choose it. You can't. You choosing to watch The Notebook is cheating.

3. I held her hand as we walked from the house. Actually, I held her hand in one hand and the pizza in the other, so it might have been the best moment ever. I could barely keep from giggling uncontrollably or like peeing myself, which are clearly both not okay to do on a date, guy or girl, doesn't matter. If you do both at the same time while you are on a date, please put down this book and talk to your doctor, you're a wreck.

So, just to outline where we were at in our relationship:

We were eating pizza, holding hands and watching the freaking Notebook.

I liked her. I wanted her to know I liked her. I needed to be bold. As the young Ryan Gosling dangled from the Ferris wheel and Rachel McAdams looked surprised, I began detailing a plan to kiss her. On the lips. Booya.

The plan was simple. I would briefly describe my thorough enjoyment of the film, validating any thoughts she may have also about the film. At that moment I will stop talking and make eye contact with her. Nothing intense, just enough to say, "hey I'm looking at you" because then I'll look at her lips. She'll follow my eyes. I'll move in and kiss her.

The movie was about halfway through when I got this far. They were paddling a boat in a lake full of swans.

"What holes had I missed?" I thought. There must be holes in my plan. Do I say something before? Something romantic? I don't know how to talk romantic. "Your house smells like fabric softener", that's kind of romantic. Who doesn't like the smell of fabric softener? No it should be about her. Something sweet but like also nonchalant. "Your face reminds me of a lion," I could say, and then I could talk about how much I liked the movie the Lion King. That's romantic right? Who doesn't love the Lion King?
What was I thinking, that's insane.

"Your hair is shiny." Girls spend a lot of money on shampoo products, why not point out the pros of their handiwork?

"You'd make a great mayor." That's sexy right?

"You have your dad's smile." Frick! Where does this stuff come from--that's such a weird thing to say to your dream girl.

The truth is I didn't want to be the guy to say she was beautiful. I knew all the guys who were always telling girls stuff about how gorgeous their eyes were or about their endless beauty. I know there's nothing wrong with telling a girl she's beautiful per se, but the idea of those words plopping out of my mouth made me hate myself. They were so clunky and unoriginal. It sounded so cheeseball. I wasn't like those guys. She knew that. I needed to be original. But maybe some things are tried and true. Maybe I should just stick to the script. Tell her face-to-face she was beautiful and kiss her. Yes that's what she'd want.

For sure.
Except what if she still thinks we are friends and I'm massively misinterpreting this whole thing? In which case I'll be left hung up to dry. But she is beautiful, she's beautiful and I like her. I like her the way you like somebody who you don't second-guess or wonder if you'll like them again tomorrow. I knew that I knew that I knew.

Brain:
I don't want to be a nuisance but I've got to
pop in for a second.

Me:
What do you want?

Brain:
I need to tell you something.

Me:
What?

Brain:
Don't do this.

Me:
Come on. Seriously? This again?

Brain:
I don't know how long I can do this. I can't
keep it all together.

Me:
Yes, you can.

Brain:
That's the thing. I can't. I can't because It
doesn't work like that. I'm trying to tell you the
best I can. To warn you. To tell you that you
are neglecting a major part of you.

Me:
What?

Brain:
You have a soul. You are more than just all of this. You haven't filled me with anything to keep you going and just it's just a matter of time.

Me:
A matter of time until what?

Brain:
I don't know. We've never crossed that bridge. I can't say for sure.

Me:
I'll be fine.

Brain:
Your thoughts and emotions are like seeds and what you plant is what grows and I'm telling you, what you've planted isn't anything worth growing.

Me:
Are you telling me what I think is wrong?

Brain:
No, no--I think you're distracted. You don't need a girlfriend. I am telling you, you can

listen or not, but I am telling you that it's a house of cards up here.

Me:
House of cards?

Brain:
Everything is *not* under control.
Me:
I am in control.

Brain:
That's what you want to believe but you are not.

Me:
I am in control.
Brain:
Listen, this is bigger than it was before. I don't want to have to tell you I told you so. I don't want you to overthink this; I actually don't want you to think at all. I just want you to get out.

Me:
I am in control.

Brain:
Just because you are in high school and it feels like the world is yours, it's not. It's bigger than you and what you do--it affects the way

you think. I can't keep pretending like this is
okay.

Me:
I am okay.

Brain:
Fine, fine--you're okay. I don't have any other
way of warning you.

Me:
Don't worry--I got this.

We'd made it to the old people in the movie.
I'd forgot why there are old people. I'd been so
nervous about the plan, my heart racing so
fast I'd forgot to pay attention to the movie.
Who are these old people? What if she wants
to talk about the old people? What if she won't
kiss me because of the old people and my
inability to know what they are doing? That'd
suck.

Something's sad. I know this because she just
said, "that's so sad".

"Crap," I thought, "what are these old people
doing? Probably dying cause they are old.
That's why it's sad. But what if it's something
else, something I missed. Did these old
people murder Ryan Gosling? I just put my

arm around her and said, "gosh I know isn't it?"

I thought about these old people murdering Ryan Gosling. What an odd plot for a romantic movie. Clearly, I know nothing about romance, I thought.

Then the credits went up. Soft music. "Oh shoot the plan!" I panicked. I had gotten distracted. I began skipping all the steps. I was off the plan. I went rogue. I'd gone into a spiral. I'd spent so much time thinking about the old people I'd forgot how to execute the plan. I turned to her without saying anything or looking her in the eyes. I said nothing, just breathed heavily like a sweaty bulldog. I moved swiftly, face down toward hers. I was rapidly losing oxygen in the descent. I held my breath, after taking in a large gulp of air, and inflating my cheeks like a kid plunging into a swimming pool.

This was not in the plan.

I firmly closed my eyes and parallel parked my lips on hers. Once I made contact I paused. Halted. Froze. Stood still lip-to-lip. After a moment that felt longer than it probably was she accepted my lips invitation. She accepted by puckering her lips and not slapping me in the throat.

I really knew she accepted because she kissed me right back.

Some people compare kissing to fireworks. But they don't know how much I love fireworks. I love them. So I will also compare this kiss to fireworks but because fireworks are the best thing ever and this was the best thing ever. Everything inside me said, "wahoo!" You know what kissing her felt like? It felt like in Mario Kart when you get the yellow star and that catchy song comes on and you rocket speed off and rainbow the crap out of everything. It felt like that.

The volume in life was turned up.

Then my phone rang.

THE HOSPITAL
FEBRUARY, *JUNIOR YEAR OF HIGH SCHOOL*

Growing up my mom had breast cancer. Twice. I don't remember because I was too young. Well, that's not actually true. I remember going to the waiting room and eating goldfish crackers out of a small paper cup, like the ones you use for water when you swallow a pill. I must have been no older than four. My sister was a baby. My grandpa would sit with us. I remember my mom had to go in for surgery. I remember I gave her a toy that I really liked so she wouldn't get bored. I remember visiting her and she had it by her bed. I knew it made a difference.

My mom survived. Twice.

This was different. My dad had never been sick. No, honestly I don't think he had ever stayed home from work. Here's what you need to know about my dad. He never yelled. Ever. He was cheerful, and caring, and sincere, and loved my mom a bunch and was the complete opposite of most my friend's dads who shouted, or whose egos got in the way, or were grumpy. Also, my dad never got sick.

I was turning onto the highway entrance. Rain was striking the windshield in consistent waves. I had left Anna in such a rush. I didn't even hang up the phone--I just put the receiver end to my chest and rubbed the side of my face. "I have to leave," I said to Anna, my words jumbling together. "Something happened to my dad."

I kept my mom on the other line as I drove.

"We were on the couch watching a movie," my mom's voice sounded far away. "He had been complaining about his stomach hurting earlier. I'm sure it's nothing but will you hurry down here?" Her voice trailed off, as if she was trying to fill silence but could think of no more words.

"Where's Christen?"

My sister was close with my dad. Not that I wasn't. But they have similar personalities. Same traits. Humor. Selflessness.

"She's here." I could hear my mom's breath stiff on the other end. The same stiffness as when you rip off a Band-Aid, as if to say, *can we get through this already.* "The doctors don't know. He's in a lot of pain so they are giving him something for it."

In a lot of pain? It sounded so foreign. I tried to imagine my dad in pain at all. Even in my imagination it was as if he were playing a character and would stop pretending to smile. Give me a nod, to say everything was really just fine--it was all just a show. Everything would be fine.

Everything would be fine.
It would be fine.
I was in control.

Me:
What's happening???

Brain:
I don't know but you need to get there as fast as possible.

Me:
What could be wrong with him?

Brain:
Could be a number of things.

Me:
Like what?

Brain:
We just need to hold it together. We'll find out
when we get there.

Me:
I don't want to see him in a hospital bed.

Brain:
I know it's weird.

Me:
What am I going to do?

Brain:
I don't know.

I parked in a garage reserved for visitors. I
wasn't a visitor. I was a son, and this was my
father. The digital clock on the dashboard said
eleven something as I turned off the engine.
This might be a late night. That was fine. For a
second I acknowledged the strange mixture of
emotions I was experiencing. For a second I
acknowledged her in my mind. Even in these
conditions my heart felt full with worry.

He was in the emergency room.

Sets of double doors opened as I approached.

I didn't want to see him. I didn't say this. But
everything in me was screaming it. My mom

met me outside the room. He was sleeping. Better not wake him. I relaxed. We'd find out more in the morning. Where was my sister? Was she in the room? Am I a bad son if I don't go in?

My mom looked tired, yet something in the way she spoke told me she probably wouldn't be sleeping much tonight. It was his kidney they thought. But couldn't be sure.

"We might be here a couple of days," she said. "Will you go home and feed Riley?"

Riley was our dog. I could do that. I could go home. I should do that.

I needed time to piece back together everything that had happened in the last few hours.

I'd left her house before we'd had time to even talk about the kiss. I'd stood and Anna had looked at me from the couch as I nodded. I'd said I had to go. My dad was in the hospital. I didn't know why. No, she didn't need to come. I should go. We would talk later I promised. Yes, when I get home.

I assumed we were in some sort of relationship now. The next step would be verbal confirmation. We'd talk when I got home. What will Blake say? I thought about calling him on the way home. I thought about telling him the whole story. He'd want to know about my dad. I should talk to her first. I needed the drive to walk through the night and put everything where it belonged.

Except, I needed to talk to her. I needed to talk.

Me:
Okay, I am in control. Everything is okay.

Brain:
I need to be honest. You are not in control.

Me:
This isn't that bad.

Brain:
You just need to slow down. You need to let everything catch up to you.

Me:
How?

Brain:
I don't know.

Me:
I don't know either.

Brain:
Take a second to think.

Me:
Think about what?

Crawling in the car, the rain pattered outside the parking garage. I stared at the hospital lights glowing out of clear glass and onto the wet streets.

Jesus was in this. I don't know if I knew it then or felt it, or in rearranging the memory in my mind I see it like examining an old photograph and noticing details never seen at the time the picture was taken.

One of the writers in the Bible writes this promise from God. It's a promise sometimes quoted without the context of the full story. Because the story is about a really, freaking horrible thing that's about to happen to His people. They are about to be exiled from their home. Destroyed by foreign armies. Crushed by oppressors. Defeated, and dragged out of their homes. Everything they used to know was gone. They are taken from their home in Jerusalem to Babylon. God tells them to make their home in this place, know he is with them and trust him because they won't be there forever. In the middle of telling them what's about to happen, he shares a promise.

He says, "For I know the plans I have for you...plans for welfare and not for evil, to give you a future and a hope. Then you will call upon me and come and pray to me, and I will hear you. You will seek me and find me, when you seek me with all your heart."

Then he says, I *will bring you back*.

I will restore you.
In the middle of this mess. There is a promise.

I saw this on the pavement as the rain shattered against the cement.

I couldn't have known it then, but disaster was coming.

I pulled out of the parking garage and called her.

THIS PART OF TOWN
FEBRUARY, *JUNIOR YEAR OF HIGH SCHOOL*

It hadn't started in my chest. That's what everybody had kept telling me. The doctors said it, the therapist said it, WebMD said it. That the feeling starts in your chest, a loss of breath like all the air in the room suddenly sped off, that you feel your stomach turn and it feels like there's a 747 landing and taking off on your chest.

Don't get me wrong. All of that came later. First, my hands went numb.

I hadn't thought of it as a warning sign as much as a side effect of walking to my car in the cold.

The minute she answered I heard it in her voice.

My hands went numb. Like my body was unable to speak and had resorted to some form of smoke signals to warn oncoming danger. I missed it. I should have listened. Should have noticed something was wrong. Later, doctors would give the appropriate

words for what was happening neurologically:
panic attack, anxiety, nervous breakdown,
heart palpitations, feelings of false reality,
acute onset panic disorder.
I didn't have a name for what I was feeling.

After my hands went numb, the top of my
head also went numb. The small spot right
above my forehead dulled, like something was
draining down my head and through my body.

Everything went flat. My vision condensed into
a two-dimensional flat image. Like I was
looking at a picture ripped out of a magazine. I
later talked to somebody who said for them it
always felt like oil was running over their
vision. I could see that. The best way I can
describe it is reality gets picked apart. The
way you see things becomes distorted and
hot. Like when the image on your TV is
buffering. The pieces all tear and bend and
fragment.

"I've just been confused lately," she spoke
softly. "I don't think I should be in a
relationship. I should have said something
tonight."

My heart turned against me.

It started a mutiny. A cue. A riot. All at once
there was a banging inside me as if my nerves

were taking to the streets and throwing rocks. That's how panic feels. Like you are being taken over. Panic enters the streets and from there it colonizes you. It starts on the fringe and moves inward. It finds a weak spot and attacks straight toward the center.

"I think we make good friends but that's about it."

My muscles gripped tight. Something in my stomach was shooting off rubber bullets. The city I was once king of had turned against me. My body was no longer mine. It had found a new leader. It was civil war. It was chaos. The highways of my brain froze in gridlock. Alarms flashed. Sirens were going off.

"I'm sorry if you thought anything different. I can see how it could feel like I led you on. Bryan? Are you still there?"

Am I still here?
That's a great question.

Everything inside me--brain, heart, and soul was in violent disturbance of an attack of anxiety. I could inhale quickly but as soon as oxygen touched my lungs they pushed it away and tried again. Over and over. Short compressed breath. Faster and faster. The walls of my car grew tight.

"I think this is what's best for both of us."

Everything inside me was shouting. We both said goodbye and I hung up the phone. I was in shock. Nausea barked at me like a raging police dog. Biting and growling. I used to be in control.

But a revolution had taken place.
The streets were filled with confused, angry, restless crowds, all the pieces of me I used to rely on now protesting against me.

I don't usually drive this part of town. It's desolate. Low income housing. Blocks of rundown plazas with nail salons, and liquor stores, and empty parking lots. Busted windows and bail bonds and pawnshops and barbershops and 24 hour diners.

The streets seem to all wind into one another. I'm driving aimlessly. I can feel my foot on the pedal, but I have no clue where to go. There's a bridge. I turn down a narrow alley towards it, and my first thought is to drive off the bridge, past the low cement walls, straight over the side, sideways into the sound. I want to be underwater. I want to be upside down. I want to drown. I want to see bubbles and hear the *whoosh* of water flooding the cracks in the car. I want to be anywhere but here. I look at the steering wheel, I imagine turning the wheel, turning it only a few centimeters, a slight rotation that drifts my trajectory straight over the edge. The lights of the hospital have gotten smaller behind me. Do I call somebody?

"No" I think. "Who would I talk to?"

I want to talk to her.

I want to convince her how wrong she is. I pull out my phone. I should call somebody. Tell them. Tell them the whole thing. I have people. People I could talk to. People who would understand, who would tell me nice things, who would say there are other fish in the sea, who would say that it's not a big deal- -these kinds of things happen. They might even tell me to suck it up. Which makes me angry. I get really angry at the imaginary people telling me to suck it up. Those imaginary people don't really know me. They don't know how bad this hurts. They don't know that I'm losing my grip on reality. They don't know that my dad's in the hospital and I just got my heart broken and that I'm completely falling apart.

My fists are pounding the steering wheel. Soft at first. Then harder. Louder. With more force. I am so pissed off. I see the bridge in my rearview mirror. I can feel blood rushing to my head and the sides of my hands begin to throb. I roll down the windows and let out a yell. My voice is strong and loud, so I yell again for no reason other than to hear it loud against the wind.

I drive past this little hole in the wall movie rental shop where her and I walked to one time to rent a movie with some of her friends. I yell at the movie rental store.

Stupid overpriced movie rental shop, take that.

I think about calling one of her friends and telling them. Maybe it was this whole, huge misunderstanding. Maybe they'll tell me not too worry. But I don't. Because I know it won't help. Because I know, deep down, that it isn't a misunderstanding. It's real.

I got my hopes up and got crushed. Shattered. Ran over. Heartbreak had always sounded so manageable. Like something that could be fixed. Like a bike chain or a flat tire or something that might take an afternoon to put back together. It had always sounded like more of an inconvenience. An irritation, but nothing that couldn't be pieced back together. But this...this didn't feel fixable. This felt unfixable. If this was heartbreak, why did it

feel less like a break and more like an amputation?
Like something was there, but now it's not.

"I am overreacting," I thought. "I'll feel better by the time I get home."

Music was playing from my speakers but it sounded like it was miles away.

Then I thought about our conversation again, driving from the hospital and saying goodbye. She'd sounded so sweet. Sincere. Sad.

"Okay," I'd said solemnly, "I understand."

But I didn't understand. I wasn't okay. I wanted to fight, to rage, to say, "I'm not giving up." To say something heroic. Something persuasive, like: "I'm coming over, I'll be right there and we'll talk this whole thing out. Because this is too important to me."

I pictured myself driving to her house, standing in the rain and saying to her face-to-face, "listen I'm not giving up on this."

Instead I'd just said, "goodbye."

Suddenly I stop the car. I'm sitting in a parking lot. I sit perfectly still, staring at the steering wheel.

My insides hurt. My chest hurts. Everything hurts. My ears hurt. WHY DO MY EARS HURT??

Me:
What's wrong with me?

Brain:
I can't get your heart to slow down. This is really scary.

Me:
What? What do you mean? Do your freaking job! Get this under control!

Brain:
I'm trying! Stop yelling at me! I'm trying but this is terrifying. Your vision is going in and out. I don't know what's going on. You're whole body is shutting off and on. Everything is all out of whack.

Me:
I'm fine! I'm fine!

Brain:
Stop breathing so hard! You'll pass out.

Me:
Why can't I feel my hands?!

Brain:
I DON'T KNOW.

Brain:
YOU ARE TRAPPED.

Brain:
YOU MESSED THIS ALL UP!

It was all good just a few hours ago. I was fine. Now, here I am sitting in a daycare parking lot. It's almost midnight.

It feels like there is this black hole inside my chest vacuuming up joy.

All the galaxies of life inside me were shrinking, stretching, into the event horizon of the black hole. My whole self, the self I knew and loved, was dissolving planet by planet. Star by star. Solar system after solar system gone one by one into this black hole. Any confidence, or purpose, or thing that made me feel alive was being sucked up.

My heart raced. My head swelled. I felt small. Like I was evaporating. My thoughts told me I was trapped. I was alone. I was sick. I was dying. I was done. I was a failure. No, worse, a total joke. A fraud. A lie. My life would end, and I would be forgotten.

Panic is a cancer that starts in the mind and spreads to the blood stream, piercing every organ it touches.

Anxiety forces you to live in its reality.

My hands were empty inside. They felt light and hollow against the steering wheel.

When I was a kid my best friend's little brother died of a brain tumor. He was five or six. We spent a lot of time in hospital hallways with each other, my friend and I. After his little brother was gone, something inside me shifted. I began to digest that if he could die, so could other people--and so could I. Slowly that *could* turned to *would* as I looked at history. Nobody lived forever. I remember sitting in a bathtub in my mom's bathroom,this realization flooding my bones that just as I was thinking then, I would be thinking as I died. I realized that the ending of everything was that it died.

Everybody, deep down, is scared of death. It's what keeps our species alive.

But the first time this fear hits you, it's paralyzing.
This is the familiar fear that flooded me in the parking lot.

Brain:
I TOLD YOU THIS WOULD HAPPEN!

Me:
Stop yelling.

Brain:
I can't stop.

Me:
I feel like the bottom just fell out of my life.

Brain:
It did.

Me:
What do I do?
Brain:
I don't know.

Me:
You're supposed to know!

Brain:
If you don't know--how am I supposed to
know?

Me:

...

Brain:
You thought you could have it all. But you can't, it doesn't work like that. You thought you would be a hero--all the things guys your age feel are promised to them as little boys-- but you won't and you're slowly realizing it. You're naïve. This is the rest of your life.

Me:
What's happening?

Brain:
Do you want me to be honest?

Me:
Wait, why wouldn't you be honest? Look at me--I'm a mess.

Brain:
You have a completely fake view of your whole life.

Me:
No, I don't.

Brain:
Listen, trust me--just because everybody gets a trophy and a pat on the back and everybody in your life has basically told you you can do whatever you want--it's a total lie. You aren't special or unique. You had this coming. You were made to believe you'd be whatever you

want to be. Have whatever you want. But you won't. It's this big lie wrapped up with Anna Sofia. Wrapped up with your dad lying on that hospital bed. You're not heartbroken because of some girl. You're heartbroken because the world isn't what you thought it was. Because you don't have control. You never had control. You can't control your own body. And you can't control me. For the first time, you are realizing you were never in control. You were raised to think everything would turn out fine. That you'd grow up to be a hero. Happily ever freakin' after. It's all garbage. You won't. It's all a lie. Imagine everything you've ever known, how you've always seen the world, and imagine it as this huge building--a skyscraper--and I want you to imagine it being demolished by explosives. Boom. Boom. Boom. You know, the ones that detonate from the bottom moving all the way to the top in huge clouds of bursting dust, floor by floor until it collapses into a heap of twisted steel and crumbled cement. That's the way you've always seen the world, collapsing in on itself. And it's going to hurt. It's going to hurt worse than anything you've ever felt. Because you liked the way you saw the world. You liked that building. You passed by it every day and knew which floor to go to if you needed answers. Now it's gone. And for a while you'll just see this rubble where a building once stood. But it won't be there anymore. You'll

have to find a new way to see the world.
Because the way you once saw it is gone.
Destroyed. Obliterated. *Kapoosh*.

Me:
I didn't ever say I wanted to be a hero.

Brain:
Trust me.

Me:
I can't trust you. You're not real. You're me.
You're my own emotions. A version of myself I
created to cope with my own lack of
understanding of anything. You're just as
messed up as I am. I can't physiologically
untangle you from me.

Brain:
This is just the beginning of peeling back the
wallpaper on your perfect little life.

Me:
I don't have a perfect life. Look at me! You
think this is perfect?

Brain:
You used to think so.

Me:
No, I didn't.

Brain:
Stop arguing--listen, you can try and hold it up, hold up the perfect wallpaper and pretend your life is everything it's always been--this awesome little, tiny world where you are awesome and you get whatever you want. But it's all a façade. You know what that means?

Me:
Yes, I know what façade means. Don't patronize me.

Brain:
Or you can let the wallpaper fall down. You can find out what's behind it--what's been hiding behind the whole time. You can explore this. Dive into it.

Me:
I feel like I'm going insane. I'm talking to myself. I am losing my grip on reality. Why didn't you tell me this would happen?

Brain:
I tried.

Me:
Why didn't I listen?

Brain:
You are stubborn.

Me:
How am I going to get through this?

Brain:
I guess we'll find out.

BREATH
MARCH, *JUNIOR YEAR OF HIGH SCHOOL*

Memories can comfort you.
They can also rip you up from the inside.

We're walking into Tolo.
Anna is wearing a short blonde wig.
I'm gripping the Tommy gun.
Tyler and Emily are trailing behind us.

We're getting pictures in front of an airbrushed
cityscape background. We're smiling with big
grins, until the hired photographer tells us to
look serious because we are ruthless
criminals. I point the Tommy gun in the air. He
shows us from behind his camera and we say
that it's the best shot.

I think I'm remembering it all right. The moving
images are getting broken the longer time
passes. The longer I look at them, the more
they disappear. The memories are heavy but
they are fracturing the longer I carry them.
The more I hold and touch and examine, the
less reliable they are getting. I can see Tyler's
face as we walk into the room, but even that is

changing. It's no longer a face but a memory
of a memory of a face.
Like a screenshot of a screenshot of a
screenshot.

I can see Anna's face but it's losing its
specifics. Part of the time I try and relive the
memory, the other time I'm trying to put it back
together.

We're sitting at round tables with thin black
tableclothes. We're holding hands under the
table. There is some kind of ice sculpture in
the far corner I keep looking at. Somebody is
telling us about a party somewhere. We don't
care. We're happy right here. We're happy.
Actually happy. I'm telling her we should
dance. We try to dance but nobody is actually
dancing. There are couples groping each
other, couples swaying too slowly and too
close. Everybody is complaining about the DJ.
They say he isn't playing anything anybody
wants. Nobody likes this song they say. I don't
think he's that bad. I think he has a tough job
to make a bunch of high schoolers happy. I
feel bad for him. Everybody wants to dance
but nobody wants to dance. Girls are taking
their shoes off and setting them by empty
chairs. They are circling up and dancing with
each other, pushing the guys to the edge. The
colored lights are spinning. The dark room is
shadows. But I am happy.

I am happy.
We are happy.

Next we are getting into the car. I am driving.
Tyler and his girlfriend are in the back seat.
We ditch out early. We make a point to say
goodbye and tell everybody we are leaving.
We're done here we say. It's not that cool we
say. The girls say they want to change their
clothes. Tyler and I say we are hungry. We
are driving. She turns on a song she wanted
to dance to but the DJ didn't play. We put the
windows down. The wind shoves itself through
the windows and onto our faces and into our
hair. We are yelling the lyrics. We are dancing
behind seatbelts. I am driving us. The night is
still young. The highway stretches through the
evergreen trees. I am the only car on this
road. I tap my brakes and the red glow fills
everything behind us.

I open the door for them. We put our name in
with the waitress. I have cash in my wallet.
Enough for this. I will pay for her. I will pick up
the check. The restaurant is nice. It's
crowded. Our table is in the back.

She tells me,
"This is so much fun."

I am peeling back layer after layer of
memories. I string caution tape around every

memory of us like a detective searching for fingerprints. I'm examining my memories under a microscope, looking for any evidence to make sense of what happened. Something to put together a theory. Any theory. Any theory other than the one that's right in front of me.

I watch it all play out.
When I lay awake at night.
All night.

Because I've stopped sleeping indefinitely. I don't even try anymore. Sometimes, I don't even put on proper sleeping attire. I just stay in my jeans. I leave my knit beanie on. I keep my shoes on from school. I sit on my bed. I play music through earbuds. I play music louder than I normally would. My ears hurt. Anything to drown out the noise around me. I hide under my hood in school. I sit on the covers of my bed, listening to the same songs and repeat the same memories in the same loop. The same pictures of her, playing in my mind. I see us eating pizza and laughing about Tolo. Laughing about what people did or said. I see us leaving. I'm driving. Tyler keeps talking about how he wants to go faster. He keeps telling me to drive faster. Speed up he says. You're driving like an old lady, he yells from the back seat. I turn up the stereo. We have nowhere to go. We aren't in any hurry. I don't speed up. I go slower. I want to enjoy the moment. I don't want it to go by too fast. I want to stop time. Because I am happy. But that's the trouble with time, you can't stop it. You can't slow it down. You can't speed it up. It's moving, moment-by-moment whether you like it or not.

When we get to her house we turn on a movie. A movie nobody cares about. We all keep talking. We talk loudly. Her mom has snacks for us. We aren't hungry but we take them anyway.

My whole body is tired.

Sometimes around 2am, when I get exhausted from feeling exhausted and not sleeping--I grab my skateboard and drive to a local community college and ride around for hours. The night air, it's always cold. I'm always cold now. I skate down long winding hills with large streetlights. I close my eyes. I go fast. Too fast. Faster than I should, or feel comfortable going. I kick hard to go faster. The fog always sits low against the pavement. I get lost in it. I fade away. The dashed yellow lines flashing by me.

I'm at her door. I'm driving Tyler and I back to my house now. We tell them we have to leave. I have a curfew. Tyler lingers behind. She walks me to the car. She's smiling. I hold her hands with my hands. Her hands fit in mine. "Tonight was great," she says. "Perfect," she says. She moves her arms up onto my shoulders, wrapping them around my head. I see her and she's smiling. We are both smiling. We are happy.

Every time, I stop the reel of memories here. I hit the pause button in my mind. I zoom in on the picture in my head. I make the image larger. Just our faces. So you can see all the pores and defects. I zoom in so far that it all gets blurry. It all turns to the same fleshy, hazy smudge. This is what keeps me awake. This is why I'm wired at 5am when I know my alarm will go off in an hour for school. It's this memory. This one place. This is why I go straight from my school back home to my headphones every day. This is the place in the crime scene that baffles me the most. I look at her face, I remember it, that night, I check for any indication of betrayal. Was all of this some sick joke? Did she know then? Was she playing with me like a killer whale plays with an innocent seal before it makes it breakfast? Why was she kissing me? Why? Why? Why?

Job in the Bible, the guy whose life hits the fan, has a line in his story where he's talking to God and he says:

"You throw me into the whirlwind
and destroy me in the storm."

Job has been through hell.
His whole world has been torn apart.
He's thrown into the whirlwind.

I am in the whirlwind. I am smack dab in the
middle of the storm. I feel it all around me.
The waves, and wind, and thrashing, and
darkness, and rain, and chaos. I get chaos.
I'm getting destroyed in the storm.
Anxiety is the crashing of waves.
Heartbreak is gale force winds.

Job, in the middle of his pain, looks face to
face with his Creator and says, "God threw me
into the whirlwind." Ever feel like God threw
you into a whirlwind? Ever feel like God is
destroying you in the storm?

A little about whirlwinds.

When the Bible was written, it wasn't written in
English. Most of the Bible was written in
Hebrew and the New Testament was written
in Greek. So when you read the words of the
Bible, they were translated into English from
an original text. Like any translation, certain
nuances can get lost in the crossover.
Sometimes certain translators have to take

into account not only the translation but also
the meaning behind the meaning of words.

It's like that with the word *whirlwind*, especially
the phrase, *throw me into the whirlwind.*

The word for wind here is the Hebrew word
ruwach.
This isn't any ordinary word.
It's a big word.

The Hebrew *ruwach* can mean three things:
wind, breath, or spirit.
In the beginning of the story in the Bible it
says,

"The earth was formless and empty, and
darkness covered the deep waters. And the
Spirit of God was hovering over the surface of
the waters."

The word for spirit is *ruwach.*

Later in the Exodus story, there is a moment
where the first human is *filled* with the spirit or
ruwach of God.

"I have filled him with the Spirit of God, giving
him great wisdom, ability, and expertise in all
kinds of crafts."

In the first instance of people filled specifically with the *ruwach* of God, it's for creativity. Creativity and *ruwach* go hand in hand. People can experience the same power, and love, and creativity that hovered over creation. That same energy can live inside a person. It's breath, and wind, and spirit.

In the book of Ezekiel there's a story about God putting back together his people. It has all this zombie imagery of skeletons going from skeletons to real people. It says:

"I will put flesh and muscles on you and cover you with skin. I will put breath into you, and you will come to life. Then you will know that I am the LORD."

This is what God does. He fills people up with *ruwach. His ruwach.* Dead things come alive. The story of the Bible is God breathing life into his creation.
We all have something dead in our life.
Something we wish was alive.
Something that needs the breath of God.

When Jesus is baptized, as he comes up from the water, the heavens open up and the Spirit of God descends or hovers over him, just as the Spirit did in Genesis. The storyteller is saying that this moment is like that moment.

What God is doing through Jesus is what God
has been doing in creation all along.
Jesus on the cross gives up his spirit or breath
in the final moments before everything goes
dark. After the resurrection, the storyteller
says that Jesus "breathes" onto his disciples
so they may receive the Holy Spirit.

Breath.
Spirit.
Wind.

The early Christians took this and said that the
same spirit that raised Jesus from the dead is
living in us. That God will give us life. That this
spirit dwells in us. It makes its home in us.
The same breath. That there is a power that
comes with the breath of God. It's the same
spirit that hovered over creation at the very
beginning. Early Christians wanted you to
catch that everything Jesus did was about a
new creation.
So when Job says he's in the whirlwind, what
he's literally saying is that he's in the middle of
ruwach. That God's breath or spirit or wind is
moving all around him. You could translate it
that God has caused Job to ride *ruwach.* It's
something he can participate in. What the
storyteller is saying is that God isn't gone.
That even when there's chaos--God meets us
in the chaos.

It says that God answers Job from the whirlwind.
In our deepest pain the Spirit is there.
Dwelling in our hurt, God answers us.

This is the power of the Gospel. That while we were sinners, Christ died for us. In the middle of our mess, God shows up and says, "I am making all things new."

In the middle of my whirlwind God would answer.
He'd been speaking the whole time--I just hadn't heard.
As the Bible would say, I didn't have ears to hear.

The writer in the book of Psalms says,

"The LORD is close to the brokenhearted;
he rescues those whose spirits are crushed."

And goes on to say,
"Create in me a clean heart, O God.
Renew a loyal spirit within me."

This is what I would need. For the *ruwach* of God to create new things in me.

When my skateboard wheels rattle against the road it drowns out everything. It's the only noise. It's all I hear. I go fast enough that my eyes water. They kick out tears. I am numb. This is the best chance I have to feel anything. Sometimes an SUV with 'security' printed on the side crawls through parking lots but they don't stop. They aren't worried about me. I wonder if I'm invisible. I wonder if I have disappeared. Do I even exist?

I am an investigator. I'm evaluating all records of every interaction we've had in the last few months for a sign. I'm interrogating every memory. I'm using forensics. I have search warrants.

I don't have anything.
I keep asking myself,

"What happened here?"

And in the background, beyond the rattle of my wheels, and the blaring of my headphones, and the chatter of my own brain--there, in the whistle of wind, in the sound of my own breath, I begin to hear a small voice saying,

"You are my child and I love you."

I begin to sense the Spirit of God hovering over.

SPANISH II
APRIL, *JUNIOR YEAR OF HIGH SCHOOL*

"I think we should film the whole thing at your house," I say to Blake, adding "I think it has to be this weekend. We could all sleep there and try and finish it all."

"I still don't get the concept," Blake says straight-faced, "how does that fit with the project?"

"I think we should just do what the sheet says," he says, lifting the paper with the project requirements boldly typed. "Let's not try and create a masterpiece. All I need is to get above an 80% and I'll pass this class. I am not trying to spend a lot of time together on this."

Sometimes you lose one thing in life--only to trip and knock everything else over too.

It's our fourth period Spanish II film project. The idea is that you film a five to ten minute movie highlighting the advanced vocabulary and grammatical feats you've accomplished over the course of the year thus far. Most of

the time they are corny basement scenes
involving giggling high schoolers in tacky
Halloween wigs asking each other where the
library is and giving directions, or pretending
to order food at a restaurant, or the more
common, cringe-worthy and overtly racist
scenes with teenagers dancing in sombreros
and thick black mustaches. You get the idea.
After we turn them in, we spend a solid week
just watching the class movies.

When our teacher passes out the single sheet
of paper describing the details of the
assignment, I lean toward Blake who's like
seven seats away behind me. I mouth, "I got
an idea."

He shrugs, as if to say, "good for you."

Sometimes pain doesn't just go inside us--it
goes through us.
Sometimes we are just conduits of cruelty.
We get hurt, only to hurt the ones we love.

You know the phrase, *hurting dogs bite*?
Well, it's a domino effect.

Our teacher tells us we can be in groups of
five or six.
The dream team.

Fourth period Spanish II is stacked.

It's me, Blake, Jake Anderson, Drew, and this kid named Keagen who will probably grow up to be some kind of super genius, but right now is going through a hilarious awkward stage where he won't say anything but quietly creates havoc. People think he's just this nice, shy kid until he takes his shirt off in art class and paints his stomach green, in the corner by himself, without the teacher noticing, and walks around the rest of the day like that, topless, with a green stomach, paint still running down his skin--until the principal yells at him in the hall. Or he'll bring a handful of stink bombs to English, line them up on his desk and set them off, simply smiling like a freakin' psychopath, sitting there in his desk while the stench fumes shoot into the classroom, while we evacuate. The teacher will be pounding on the outside window, and Keagen will still be sitting there, clouds puffing into the air, he'll just give this big cheesy Keagen grin and wave at her. He'll lower his head, puffs of nasty stink all around him, and he'll just keep reading *The Old Man and the Sea* like a boss.

You can see why we love Keagen.
He's a silent assassin of mayhem.

The project is worth a big percentage of this semester's grade. I don't know how grades work. Or percentages. I literally have no idea how well I'm doing in any particular class. We have basically two weeks to pull off the film.

We circle our chairs in the back of the classroom. Everybody knows Blake has the highest grade in this class, so we automatically look to him as the leader. I don't even make eye contact with him. He has his binder on his lap and writes each of our names in the corner left of his notebook paper, then writes IDEAS at the top.

"I got something," I say to the group, "it's sorta weird though."

Everybody knows I haven't been myself. They can smell it like sharks on blood. They all sit a little further back. Like whatever I am feeling is contagious. They stop trying to get me anywhere on Friday nights. They stop texting me. Except Blake. He'll swing by the house, I am pretty sure just to check on me, but he'd never say that. He used to swing by. He doesn't anymore.

Nobody acknowledges her either. They kind of pretend like it never happened. Except Blake. A couple weeks ago he sat by me in the hall. I was wearing the shirt from the concert like some schmuck, and he sat down next to me as groups trolled by holding their backpack straps or carrying books, and he said he'd heard what happened. He said he was sorry to hear about it.

"That sucks," he said. "But whatever."

I didn't say anything. I just sat there wearing that dumb brown shirt. I didn't even know why I wore it to school. I guess I thought it would be heroic. Like I was saying I didn't care what happened by wearing it. But wearing it only made everything worse. It wasn't even my size. It was too small. I felt gigantic in it. It was the middle of winter. I was freezing.

"Are you depressed?" Blake asked point blank.

"I think so," I said, staring at the wall in front of me. "I am not sure."

"I think you are."

"How?"

"I just know." He said, "we've been friends since kindergarten--you're lousy at hiding your emotions. You know what you need to start with? You need to stop listening to the same depressing music."

"I am not." I lied.

"You're lying, you always do that when something like this happens, and you always listen to depressing music and watch depressing movies and stay up too late..."

"Not like this," I interrupted. "This is different. This really sucks."

"I know, I just..."

"You don't know!" I blurted, finally turning to face him. "You have a girlfriend. You are going to finish this conversation and go back to your girlfriend--you have only ever had *one* girlfriend. You and Holly--the perfect couple. You have *no* idea how I'm feeling." My face was turning red, I could feel it, and I said, "You don't have any idea because you and Holly-- you wouldn't understand because you are stuck in your own world."

"What's that supposed to mean?"
"It means both your parents are rich. You guys just do whatever you want and don't care and plus she's so... so *simple*."

"*Simple*?"

I'd only seen Blake's face like this a handful of times. He looked like his dad. His face was firm. His dad once told us a story about how his business partners had tried to go behind his back and screw him over in court. When he told us the story of what happened in the courtroom his face got all tight, his chin sticking out, like Blake's was now.

"You've said it before yourself," I said, trying to retreat, "that she's just *simple.* It's not like I said she was stupid."

"No, what I said was that when it comes to choosing a college *her perspectives are simple.* I *never* said she was simple. I would never say that. Is that what you think? That Holly is stupid? No, you know what, I know you do. You could never be happy for me. You always have to undermine her. Sorry she's not some hip, trendy, too-cool-for-school, indie girl. No, you know what, I am not sorry because at least she won't stomp on my heart or lead me on or dump me on a whim. You're a horrible person when you get like this. If you want to be depressed that's fine, that's your choice, mope around, and feel sorry for yourself, but you stepped into an oncoming train on this one. Dude, I came by your house because your mom called my mom--she said she was worried you don't have any friends anymore. That you basically sit in your room and do nothing. I am your *one* friend in all this. But, I won't pity you, or let you act like this. You're a bigger person than this, at least that's what I thought. The best friend I have wouldn't let this overtake him. He wouldn't mope around. If you really are depressed go see a doctor. Go get a therapist. Go to the gym. Get a puppy. Get medicine. Ride a bike. Do whatever it takes. Pick up a new hobby. Fight to get your life back. Pick yourself up, dust yourself off and get back to being yourself. But stop pretending your life is some tragedy. Stop acting like some wounded martyr. You're not."

Now he was standing, getting his backpack and swinging it over his shoulder. He was standing above me. I felt small. I felt tiny.

"I remember last year, when you told me you wanted to be a youth pastor. You said, I remember, you said 'God told you... *called* you to it.' If you are called stop acting *uncalled*. You said God had a plan for your life--well, if that plan was true then it's still true now. Stop trying to un-plan what God planned. You can be sad. But stop acting like this is the end of the world. Stop cutting out all the people who love you. I remember riding in the car with you and you telling me about Jesus and I believed what you were saying. I believed that God was really changing the way you see things and it began to change me, but when you pull crap like this I wonder-- not about God, but about how small you've made him. I'm not perfect and I am not good at God stuff, if I'm being honest, I really suck at it--but I think you believe in a God that's bigger than this. I get that you got hurt. I get that this hurts, but I promise you that God *hasn't* given up on you. You've given up on you. I think you are a bigger person than this. I don't know what's happened to you this year. I don't know why you don't talk to me or why you are alone all the time or why you got obsessed with this freakin' girl, dude, I don't know why your dad got sick--but I know that I am your friend and I won't throw a good friendship away for this."

Blake turned his head, looking straight at me, as if he could see beyond the mask I was hiding behind. His eyes said that he really did feel deep sympathy for me, maybe not my situation but for me.

"You're being a jerk," he said. "I don't know why, when all I've done is stick up for you behind your back."

Then he walked away, down the hall, and around the corner.

I realized the hall was empty. The bell had already rung. I'd be late. There was a small freshman jogging past me, clearly also late.

That was the last time Blake and I had really talked.

"So what's your idea?" Jake says.

Blake has his mechanical pencil pressed to the page and he's staring at me. Everybody is staring at me. Right as I begin to speak I'm interrupted by a loud,
"TIME IT!" from Drew, who just as quickly flips around to see the face of the large clock hanging over the window.

"ELEVENTWENTYSIX!" Shouts Jake.

Our teacher gives us a nasty stare from her desk.

Every day, right around eleven thirty our principal, Mr. Slavsky uses the faculty bathroom across from our Spanish II classroom. Slavsky is a bear of a man. He's burly and Russian, and has a powerful mustache. We're talking like a megalomaniac motherland Soviet Russia communist stash. The thing has probably killed people with household items. I'm pretty sure his mustache started the Cold War. If he has super powers, or secret spy documents, or Skittles--I'm pretty sure they are all hidden in that epic stash.

We have a perfect view of the faculty bathrooms from our desks in class. As soon as Slavsky closes the door to the bathroom we yell, "TIME IT!"

Doesn't matter if we are in the middle of a lecture, or exam. Doesn't matter what's happening. Once it's been yelled, Jake gets out *The Log*. *The Log* is both a series of notebook pages with start and finish times for Slavsky's daily dumps and it is a fantastic pun. *The Log*. You're rolling your eyes. Get over it, it's genius and you know it.

Slavsky has some really admirable times saved over the course of the year. The longest, recorded in October--was a fifty-one minute dump. It was glorious. When he strolled out, wiping his hairy tsar hands on the sides of his slacks, we all stood and cheered.

Another time, in mid January, Slavsky had been in for around twenty minutes when Keagen quietly got up in the middle of class and walked out. We could see him walk across the hall to the bathroom. Our teacher was looking at us and said, "Where is Keagen going?" We shrugged and were like, "Ummm how can we know what goes on inside his head?"

Keagen gently knocked on the door--Slavsky answered it, towering above Keagen and as Keagen told us later, he said to Slavsky, "Do you have any gum?"

Slavsky told him to get back to class.

Keagen told Slavsky he should carry around gum, to help create a "more approachable image with the student body."

After that, Keagen was a legend.

Today, Jake gets *The Log* out and records the time.

Everybody turns back to me. I say I have an idea for our movie, I say it's about a guy, and I try to explain it but it all spills out wrong. "Where's the Spanish?" Blake says, tapping his mechanical pencil against the notebook.

I don't know where the Spanish is.
I don't know what the point is either.
 "I am down with whatever." Drew says.

Blake asks, "Does anybody have anything better?"

Nobody responds.

"Okay, looks like that's it," Blake says, more to me than anybody else. "Everybody can come over to my house this weekend. We'll start putting this together."

Right then Jake yells, 'ELEVENFORTYNINE!'

Slavsky walks out, shutting the door behind him.

Blake looks at me in a way that isn't hate or appreciation or forgiveness, but a look that says,

"We'll see."

It's not hope, it's not regret--but it's the start of something new.

PSALMS
APRIL, *JUNIOR YEAR OF HIGH SCHOOL*

I've moved my mattress right by my window. I keep the window open day and night, sleeping with a winter sleeping bag I found in the basement. It's blue and puffy, and smells like old things and dust. I keep a wool beanie on for extra warmth. I am writing over and over the concept for our Spanish video. I pour over it. At first, the whole thing is just about one guy, and it follows him through a full day. Then it becomes more complex. More characters. Flashbacks. This guy's full history. I write the whole thing on notebook pages in black ink. It's the story of a guy who is trying to participate in normal interactions while feeling like he's walking through a dream. He has flashbacks to a war he never fought in. He gets in fistfights with people he doesn't know, then wakes up in the woods. He dances at a party only to wake up alone beside the edge of a swimming pool.

It's Friday evening. We'll begin filming tomorrow morning bright and early at Blake's house. Blake lives in a large lodge style mansion, at the top of a long wooded driveway. The house has a full size taxidermy stuffed brown bear standing upright, a wine cellar, a gun cellar, and ski resort décor. It has an outdoor swimming pool with boulders lining the edges. There's a sauna. There is a theater room upstairs. My favorite is the hidden bedroom behind a bookcase. It's where I always sleep--it feels so safe and hidden. Except, there's a bunch of mouse traps because Blake says mice live back there.

I'm supposed to finish the script, that's my job. My family isn't home yet. Christen is at a friend's for the weekend. My parents aren't home from work. I'm by myself. The house is quiet minus the droll of the furnace. I've been in a fury of writing down thoughts. I haven't *actually* written a line of Spanish, mostly because I don't know any Spanish--at least, not as much as I should by Spanish II. To be fair, our Spanish II teacher left last year and they weren't able to replace her so we have a young English teacher, Ms. A, pinch-hitting. I certainly don't know enough Spanish to adequately portray the complex story and emotions I'm trying to convey in this project. I see the scenes in my mind and try to convey them with body language or song ideas I've written in the margin to play alongside the scenes. At my last count the movie could be twenty minutes. We'll have to cut that down. I figure I'll go back through and add the

Spanish words we are supposed to have for credit. Maybe dub them over. I don't have time for that now.

Spanish II has no idea what's about to hit it.

Everybody else is trying to make their little five minutes of dialog.

I'm making a masterpiece.
I'm creating a magnum opus.

I feel like I can be real, and it's overpowering. There's beauty in being real. Being real, for everybody to see, is you saying *me too*. When you have the courage to be vulnerable, to split yourself open, to show who you are--flaws and all, you give the world a chance to say, *me too*. It's a gift. Everybody feels alone. Having the courage to show everybody who you are gives them the power to be who they are. Exactly where they are.

That's the power of honesty.

I'd begun to realize that I was hiding behind a mask.

God has a way of helping us be the *real* us. He's beside us, a few steps ahead, leading us forward into His love and peace and grace and purpose--reminding us to take off the mask.

My guess is you have a mask.

The Bible says that God created us in His image. We aren't our own tiny gods. We have a spark, a stamp, a surge of the divine, of God within us. It's the real us. The honest us. The us that matters. There's something that happens when we invite God to begin working in us--when we invite the power of Jesus to take us over--that he begins to show us who we really are.

I hadn't prayed a magical prayer.
Or said the right words.
Or proclaimed just the right things in the right order.

My heart was in the right place.
I didn't just need Jesus as an idea.
I needed Jesus as the only thing in my life.

When you hit rock bottom--when the floor falls out on your life, you realize what's the most important.

In the Bible there is a book about being real. About saying all the things you really want to say. It's about looking at God and expressing

what's inside. All the messy, ugly, angry,
anxious fragments of us we want to hide.

It's the book of Psalms.

I think we think following Jesus means you're
perfect.
It's not.

It's about being real. More real. It's poetry. It's
song lyrics. The angst of the broken hearted.
It was exactly what I needed. One Psalm
says,

"The ropes of death entangled me;
  floods of destruction swept over me.
The grave wrapped its ropes around me;
  death laid a trap in my path.
But in my distress I cried out to the LORD;
  yes, I prayed to my God for help.
He heard me from his sanctuary;
  my cry to him reached his ears."
This writer--thousands of year before me was
going through what I was going through. It
was a giant billboard saying *me too*. It was
this person, thousands of years before me,
being real with where they were at, saying,
"I've suffered, and God heard me right where I
was", and I felt like they were talking to me.
That's the power of the words in the Bible--
they can feel like they are written just for you.

I go upstairs and sit on the couch to brainstorm, and that's when it happens.

I feel the spiral of anxiety. The sadness--it's all at once like a punch in the gut. The living room is dark. I try to turn on music to settle myself. I walk to the kitchen. I get a glass of water. I drink slowly. My face is hot. The room spins.

Brain:
EVERYTHING IS FALLING APART!

Me:
I know, I know, I know--I'm trying to keep everything together.

Brain:
YOU CAN'T!

Me:
I can!

Brain:
YOU ARE WORTHLESS!

Me:
It's going to be okay.

Brain:
NO! IT WON'T! THIS WILL NEVER END!
THIS IS THE REST OF YOUR LIFE! YOU
ARE A MESS!

Me:
I am a mess!

I sit down at the kitchen table. The aloneness
clutches me in its mouth the same way grizzly
bears bite down on a struggling salmon
shaking to get free.

Brain:
YOU ARE A MISTAKE!

Brain:
YOU ARE ALONE!

Brain:
YOU ARE HEARTBROKEN!

Brain:
YOU ARE AFRAID!

I don't know what to say back. My thoughts
attack me. I have no words to say back to
them. Maybe, because I know they are right.
Or I believe them. I am not in control. I was
never in control. It's just what I told myself to
hide all the things I didn't want to
acknowledge happening inside of me. Not

being in control is a scary thought, and now--
now, this happens more than I'd like it to. This
happens where my brain begins to speak so
fast I can't catch up. My thoughts yell at me. I
get sad, then I get scared, then I get all
screwed up with my heart racing, then I lose a
grip on what's real. I don't have anything I can
do. That's what it feels like. Right there in the
kitchen, from somewhere else, not me or my
brain or my own thoughts--but somewhere
deep in my soul, a small whisper. A tiny tug on
my heart. A quiet nudge. Like a friend who
hasn't said anything in a crowded room for a
long time, then in a hushed voice says, "Sup."

"For God gave us a spirit not of fear but of
power and love and self-control."

It's a scripture I had memorized a long time
ago. I stop and try and feel it. Power and love
and self-control. I have power and love and
self-control. Not my brain. *Not you, brain.* I do.
Power and love and self-control. I repeat them
to myself. To my thoughts. Try and absorb the
truth behind every syllable. God gave me not
a spirit of fear but of power.

Of love.

And self-control.

I have a God who hasn't abandoned me. It's the first time I've thought this in a long time. I could feel guilty about this but I don't--I don't because I trust the power of the cross. I trust that when Jesus said he'd always be with us, he meant it. I trust that when Jesus was on the cross and he looked over all of creation and quotes a Psalm, saying, "My God, my God, why have you forsaken me?" he was taking our anxiety and pain and sin on himself and feeling it--experiencing it.

The cross is a billboard of *me too*.
It's Jesus saying you aren't alone in this.

Brain:
NOBODY LIKES YOU!

Brain:
YOU'RE A MISTAKE!

Brain:
EVERYTHING ABOUT YOU IS WRONG!

I breathe. I slow down. I imagine Jesus, I imagine him feeling anxiety. My anxiety. And a Psalm, a Psalm from somewhere far off comes into my head and I begin to say it to myself. To my spinning mind. And it does something. It's Psalm 40--a Psalm my mom used to say out loud when we were little and she had breast cancer. When the hospital bills piled up on the kitchen counter and my grandparents came to live with us to help around the house and she was sick. Very, very sick. It's a song. An anthem. A refuge.

Brain:
YOU ARE FALLING APART!

Brain:
YOU ARE A FAILURE!

Me:
I waited patiently…

Brain:
YOU ARE ALONE!

Me:
…for the LORD to help me, and he turned to me and heard my cry.

Brain:

…

Me:
He lifted me out of the pit of despair, out of the mud and the mire.

Brain:

…

Me:

He set my feet on solid ground and steadied me as I walked along. He has given me a new song to sing, a hymn of praise to our God.

Brain:

....

Me:

Many will see what he has done and be amazed. They will put their trust in the Lord.

The writer in the book of Hebrews says that the words written in the Bible are,

"Living and active and sharper than any two-edged sword, and piercing as far as the division of soul and spirit."

The words from the Psalmist pierced into my soul and spirit, and in this moment are words that give me peace. Give me a spirit not of fear--but power and love and self-control.

Everything around me calms. I can feel my hands again. I feel my feet on the ground. The glass of water. The sound of the house's heater lulling. I sense that Jesus is with me. I don't know how to describe this, and I know some of you might not believe me--or will say it was just a sudden rush of blood to the head, or my imagination--but there's something that

I can only describe as Jesus, with me, in me, alive, breathing life into me.

Saying *me too.*

I walk back to the living room and sit on the couch beside my pile of scribbled notes. They can wait I think. I feel less anxious, but I still feel sad. I stare at the wall. The front door swings open so fast my blood pressure blasts again and my heart races. It's my dad, home from a day in the office. He walks in with his laptop in hand and his empty coffee cup that he always takes to the office. He pauses in the doorway. He looks at me on the couch. He must be able to see it all over me. The notebook pages beside me, the skin on my face red, heart racing, sadness written in my eyes. He asks,

"Are you okay?"

GOOD FATHER
APRIL, *JUNIOR YEAR OF HIGH SCHOOL*

"You're sitting here with all the lights off on a Friday night listening to really depressing music."

My dad walks into the living room flicking on the light switch, spilling warmth, and threatening light into the room.

There, back in the hospital, my mom had called to let me know that my dad would be okay. He was passing a gallstone. A large and very, very painful gallstone. I asked my mom what that meant and shuddered--wishing I hadn't asked. But, he would live. He would be okay. I didn't realize the stress that had been sitting on my shoulders. The angst that fluttered off when I heard the news.

There in the living room, my dad--he's wearing his typical collared shirt and slacks. His laptop briefcase is tucked under his arm with his coffee cup hanging from his thumb. He has bags under his eyes. He looks at me and around the dark room. I feel exposed. I wonder if he's going to lecture me. I feel like

I'm letting him down. I don't want to look him in the eyes. I want to hide. I want to be alone. "Shouldn't you be with your friends tonight?" he says, trotting beside me and into the kitchen. The clank of his coffee mug in the sink, the faucet hisses, water splashes against the hollow inside as he washes it out and sets it on the counter. The heels of his dress shoe boom on the hardwood floors.

"I'm working on a Spanish project."

I pick up the stack of loose-leaf notebook pages as evidence, holding them above my head so he can see from the kitchen.

———————

There's a story Jesus tells about a son.

He's telling it to a crowd of religious people.

He starts the whole thing off by saying that there is this son who says to his dad, "Give me my inheritance."

That's how the story starts.

Jesus tells the crowd that he is the younger of two sons.

This son goes to his dad and basically says, "I wish you were dead; give me everything you are worth or you were planning to give me when you died."

He says, "I want it all right now."

It's the middle finger to a father who loves him.

It's an incredibly hurtful act.

I'm sure the crowd around Jesus was appalled. In their culture the father of a household was to be respected. He was to be honored. Something like this was a big deal. It wasn't just rebellious, it was tearing his family apart. The son wasn't just defiant--he was disregarding his father all together. He was saying, *you mean nothing to me, except whatever you have to give me.*

It's a heartbreaking scene.

The dad gives everything to his son. The son takes all the money and leaves. Packs up his stuff and takes off. Jesus says that this son travels far away from home. He leaves his family. Once he gets far enough away, he parties. Like seriously parties. He goes hard. He lives fast. Jesus says that he lives *recklessly*. He spends all of his inheritance on himself.

Somewhere far from home, the son is left broke and broken.

He's alone.

"This son," Jesus says, "gets the only job he can, feeding pigs."

You can imagine the faces of the religious people around him grinning, nodding, and appreciating the story Jesus is telling. *Finally,* they think, *this idiot, dumb freaking kid is getting what he deserves.*

The crowd begins to stir with satisfaction. You disrespect the father, your life falls apart. That's what justice looks like. End of story. Good story, Jesus.
Jesus adds that the younger son gets so desperate to eat--he's so hungry--that he'd settle to eat the food the pigs were eating, but they wouldn't give him any.

When you have nothing, you have nothing to lose.

When you are empty, you'll grab at anything to feel full.

The religious guys around Jesus were probably laughing at this point. It's a great touch to the story. Because for them--the way they saw the world, there were bad people and good people, and they were the good people, and the bad people were always left broken and alone. That's the way the world worked.

But Jesus isn't done with his story. He says that the son decided to go back home because even his dad's employees were better off than he was. He starts this whole speech about how he's sinned against his dad and if he could just be brought on as the lowest employee, if he could just work the rest of his days for his father, he'd be able to live. He says, "I don't deserve to be called a son."

So he travels all the way back home.

The walk of shame.

The religious crowd knows how this should go. The son should approach his father's house only to be turned around by his father's servants. Seen from a mile away and dismissed. He should be shooed off. Spit on. Actually, he should be happy just to leave with his life. No respectful Jewish man would even speak or show himself to a son like this.

They're shaking their heads at this son--why even go back?

Jesus' story says,

"When he was still a long way off, his father saw him. His heart pounding, he ran out, embraced him, and kissed him. The son started his speech: 'Father, I've sinned against God, I've sinned before you; I don't deserve to be called your son ever again.'"

The dad says,

"My son is here--given up for dead and now alive! Given up for lost and now found!"

See, this isn't a story about a son--it's a story about a good dad. Jewish men didn't run in that culture. Running was for kids. But this dad is so excited to see his son back home, he sprints to his son. The dad sees his son somewhere way down the road, and he stops what he's doing and runs towards this son. This son who messed everything up.

This is the story Jesus decides to tell to describe God.
A story about a dad who drops everything to run toward his son who's returning home.

My dad is standing beside the couch and he says,

"You don't have any plans tonight but working on your Spanish project?"

I tell him it's a really big project. I say that I'm putting all my creative energy into it. I say I have to be alone to think. It's more than a *have* it's a need. I need to be alone. These words sink into me. Because they are true. Ever since that night I've needed to be alone.

In the Genesis poem--after God creates people, or *a* person to be more specific--he looks at him and he has this line, he says, "man isn't meant to be alone."

And it's true.

When I am alone, I realize I make everything about me.

In tenth grade we had to read *Of Mice and Men* for English--there was a part that always stuck out to me:

"A guy needs somebody—to be near him. A guy goes nuts if he ain't got nobody. Don't make no difference who the guy is, long's he's with you. I tell ya, I tell ya a guy gets too lonely an' he gets sick."

I think of my dad, sitting there on the couch, he can see this *sick* all over my face.

"If you don't have plans," my dad says, "let's go for a drive."

I ask where. I ask why. I ask what is he talking about. I've never just gone for a drive just to drive around. My dad doesn't go for drives just to drive around. This isn't a thing.

"You need to get out of the house," he says, "and it's better than just sitting here."

"Where are we going to go?"

"Where do you want to go?"

"Far from here," I reply quickly without thinking over the words. I expect my dad to be surprised by my response but he isn't. He doesn't look shocked or scared or even disturbed. He shrugs in his dad way and says,

"That sounds good to me."

There's a brand new suspension bridge project opening a second bridge beside an original. It's about an hour drive. My dad's heard the cables are now illuminated with lights and the towers have been completed.

He says we should drive over the original
bridge and check out the new one.

I sit in the passenger seat; we pull out of the
driveway and cruise out of the neighborhood.
Neither of us say anything.
Jesus says in his story that this dad, the dad
whose son left, he throws a party for his son.
He accepts the son back into the family. It's a
welcome home party. That's what God does.
He throws us a party. Jesus says that God
isn't into I told you so's, but is more interested
in throwing parties.

From the car my Spanish project leaves my
mind. I sit still. We drive towards the city. We
drive past towns. We drive further out from our
house. Far away. Past mile markers, and
hillsides, and spanning on through the
distance it feels like we stretch through time,
past cities and centuries, to a place
somewhere in the future.

My brain is quiet. It's peaceful in the car. The
highway streetlights whizzing by my window.
For the first time I feel like I can think. I can
just be.

My grandfather's words pop into my head,

"The story isn't over."

My story isn't over.
My dad has the radio on low in the background. I can pick up the faint cry of a pop song. The road bends along a wide bay of water holding far off ships with orange lights. Above are the constellations, orbits of satellites, the distant spark of far off galaxies.

Junior year has been--I realize stubbornly, a series of me *pretending*--pretending to be okay, pretending to be in control, pretending to follow Jesus--while simultaneously putting other things in front of him, as more important than him. I put my status above him, I put my grades above him, I put myself above him, and I put my relationship with Anna above him.

All of it I put above God.

In the Exodus story in scripture it says God hears the cry of his people. He heard them and he rescues them. Redeems them. Delivers them from slavery. God leads them into the wilderness and it's there that he says,

"I am the Lord your God, who brought you out of the land of Egypt, out of the house of slavery. "You shall have no other gods before Me."

The wilderness is a scary place. It's the place of the unknown. His people have been slaves in a far away place. God tells them he will take them home, to this place he promised them would be their home--but they have to trust him and only him. He's going to be the only God they have.

Back in Egypt, the Egyptians didn't have one god--they had a bunch of gods. Their concept of God was a lot of gods. There wasn't just a sun god, and animal gods; there were also gods for your particular neighborhood. Local gods. People would worship one god but also sacrifice to a few other gods, just to be safe.

So when God takes the Israelites out of Egypt--he makes a point that they will only worship him. He is the one true God. He is the God who showed up to Moses at the burning bush. He is the God who created everything. There aren't other gods, there is just him. He is the one true God. The God of their ancestors. The God that had been fighting for them the whole time. If he didn't make it clear--the Israelites would get distracted. They would put other things in front of him. You can take the Israelites out of Egypt but then you have to take the Egypt out of the Israelites.

God doesn't just want to be the chief God in a lineup of other gods --he doesn't want to share the stage with anything else in his people's hearts. That's the whole thing. It's a relationship. It's a covenant. Nobody wants to be cheated on. God doesn't want part of our lives--he wants the whole thing. That's what worship is. You hand over your soul. You give over your heart. You take the keys out of the ignition and hand them over. God was leading his people into the unknown but first they had to put him first. God had to be above all else in their lives.

There's a truth to how this works because the more you turn your focus to God the less you're focused on yourself. You let go of all the things weighing you down.

Sitting in the car I realized what I'd done. I'd put a lot of things above where God was. All my thoughts, energy, and time were concerned with *myself*. I was filling my need for God with all these other things.

I was in the unknown. I was in the wilderness. I needed to not just say I believed in God, but I actually needed to trust that he was good.

As the two bridges approach in front of us, the giant pillars, bright lights, cables, and fresh pavement--I look over at my dad, his eyes are fixed on the road.

You might not have had a good dad. You might not have a dad who saw you at your worst and took you on a drive, but that's okay. You have a good dad in heaven that is taking you places even at your worst.

God's a good father--I'd traveled to a faraway place without realizing it. I'd lived recklessly in my own heart. I was the son far away. I was the one who'd left.

The whole time, I'd been wondering where God was but it was me who was gone. It was me who walked away. It was me who'd packed up and left.

I'd made so many little choices that got me so far from home. My anxiety was spilling out of a soul that was restless. A heart that was unfulfilled. Because all the things I'd made my gods--they made pretty terrible gods. Terrible gods make even worse saviors.

The book of Proverbs in the Bible, the writer says to,

"Guard your heart above all else, for it determines the course of your life."

We drove up over the old bridge and beside it--a new cement structure- a bridge at least twice the size of the original. Wide, curved cables, giant oblong shapes, the white lights of the night road crews high above the water bellow. My dad slowed as we drove parallel to

it. The cement seemed to glow against the
blue ocean stretched along the horizon.

Me:
The story isn't over.

Brain:
Is everything going to be okay?

Me:
Yes. Yes, I think so.

Brain:
What about all that stuff that could go wrong?

Me:
It's all still there. It all could still suck. But I
need you to hear this--I need you to hear that I
have a God that's for me. I am not alone.

Brain:
But...

Me:
No, you don't decide anymore.

Brain:
What if...

Me:
No, I'm going to be okay.

Brain:

...

Me:
It's all going to be okay.

Brain:
But...

Me:
"For I know the plans I have for you... they are plans for good and not for disaster, to give you a future and a hope."

Brain:

...

Me:
That's how we are going to work now.

Brain:
Okay--I get it.

Me:
Good.

This is what coming home feels like. It feels like confetti cannons, and liftoff, and beats dropping to packed dance floors, and new shoes, and home cooked food, and redemption, and courage, and grace, and death getting dropkicked in the neck, and hope flexing it's muscles, and a party, and love.

Coming home feels like love showing up.

In the wilderness, when God's people are facing the unknown, scripture says,

"Be strong and courageous. Do not fear... for it is the Lord your God who goes with you. He will not leave you or forsake you."

God was building a new bridge in me. I was crossing over from fear into faith. From slavery to a Savior. A bridge from anxiety to trust.
Lost and found.

A miracle and a metaphor.

THE FUTURE
TEN YEARS AFTER JUNIOR YEAR OF HIGH SCHOOL

I've been writing to you this whole time but haven't told you much about who I am here ten years after high school, so I'd like to formally introduce myself before it's too late. After Junior year I made it through my Senior year and graduated high school. I moved out and went to college. Blake and I lived together in college in an apartment, then a house, then back into an apartment.

Brain:
Tell them about… *you know*.

Me:
Dude chill, I am getting there.

Brain:
Okay. Just wanted to make sure. You are forgetful.

Me:
I know, *I know*, but I got this dude.

Brain:
By the way, I'm not being nitpicky but you
went to community college, not *college*
college.

Me:
That's college.

Brain:
I mean, I get that--but you're making it sound
like you went to MIT.

Me:
Why you gotta do me like that? Fine, yes--I
went to community college. I apologize if that
was misleading. Anything else?

Brain:
Nah, you're good.

Me:
May I proceed?

Brain:
You don't have to get an attitude; I'm just
trying to make sure you aren't lying.

Me:
Alright, *alright*--thank you for your input.

Brain:
Welcome.

After *community* college and after getting a first job--I met Kayla Rae.

Brain:
Annnnndd…. Who's that?!?

Me:
I am getting to it--calm yourself.

I met Kayla Rae--who is beautiful the way a girl is beautiful who is fully living out what God created her to be. She is fearless, and transparent, and saucy, and loving. She's a boss, and pretty, and selfless, and kinda gangster, and in love with Jesus.

But, before I get any further--hear this, before I asked Kayla out on a date--I had a job, and I was fine being single. This is huge. I was cool with who Jesus was in my life. I was content with that.

So, I asked her on a date.

A few months later I called Blake on my way to work. He was working in San Diego for a company he helped start.

"I am going to marry this girl."

"How do you know?"

"When you know," I said, "you just straight up know. Like you can feel it."

"I can hear it in your voice."

"What?"

"That you are going to marry her."

"What do I sound like?"

"Like your going to marry her."

"What does that sound like?"

"Like you know what you're going to do and you're going to do it."

"I don't know," I said, half remembering all the stuff we'd been through in sort of a sweeping of memory and gravity of nostalgia, "it's crazy cause you kind of don't really think that one day you'll just find somebody who you'll be like--*you and me until death do we part*--and I think it should freak me out. Like, I should be like *oh shoot*--you know, but I am not. I am not at all. It sounds crazy, but I'm like let's go for this. Like this is the next chapter and I know it."

"That's really good news!"

"Thanks."

"I am serious--this is really, really good news and I am really happy for you. This is a big deal."

It was a big deal.

Months later I asked Kayla to marry me. We were on a pier and the waves were crashing below us, I buckled down, my back hunched and I asked her. She said yes and on the way home--in the car I called Blake to tell him and I ask him to be my best man.

Standing there on my wedding day--Blake standing on my right and my bride to be at the end of the long aisle, her arms tucked in her dad's, and with large, round, happy tears inching down her cheeks--I understood something new. I understood God in a new way. My heart was dance fighting in my chest. And my vomit control team inside my stomach was like, "we're doing the best we can down here--but you're going to have to focus in because this could go either way." I knew this is what in the Bible the writer John meant when he said that one day, that there would come a day that all of creation would be like a bride meeting her husband when God makes his home here for good, and evil, and death are conquered.

In that moment, at the end of the aisle, reaching for her hand and nodding to her dad in a look that was sentimental but also like, "you still cool with this?" I looked Kayla in the eyes and I experienced this rhythm of grace, this drumbeat of joy, this colossal movement of forever kind of love parading within my soul.

This is the kind of language the writers of the Bible choose to use when talking about forever with our creator.

A wedding day. A bride meeting a groom. Jesus and the church. A creator and creation. God and his people. God will make his home here.

For anybody who's always heard that eternity will be us somewhere else, up in the sky playing harps--this isn't the story the writers of the Bible talk about. The story they tell is that God will make his home here with us and we will spend forever loving, creating, and celebrating with our God.

Forever isn't far up in the clouds.

It's here.

When you chose to be a part of God's kingdom heaven starts now and just keeps going on into forever. That's the choice you get. You get to choose to start heaven now and bring heaven here or if you choose, to put everything else in the place of God and put yourself first and to me that sounds a lot like hell. You get that choice. Forever with our creator is grace colliding with all of creation. And it's a moment that I think I have a tiny glimpse of. A moment with my bride and my family and friends, I think that's what our future will feel like with Jesus.

Only bigger.
And better.

That's what we have to look forward. Paul says in his letter to the Romans,

"For all creation is waiting eagerly for that future day when God will reveal who his children really are."
He goes on to say,

"Creation looks forward to the day when it will join God's children in glorious freedom from death"

Will things be easy? Probably not. But easy isn't the goal. Life with Jesus is the goal. Loving others is the goal. Seeing God's kingdom here is the goal.

When anxiety or depression tries to stick its head up into my life this is what I remember--I remember what Paul wrote to his close friends in Corinth in his letter, he says that he has this struggle, he doesn't mention what *the struggle* is but he calls it a *thorn in his flesh.* For me, it's anxiety or depression. Listen to what he says,

"I begged the Lord to take it away. Each time he said, 'my grace is all you need. My power works best in weakness.' So now I am glad to boast about my weaknesses, so that the power of Christ can work through me. That's why I take pleasure in my weaknesses, and in the insults, hardships, persecutions, and troubles that I suffer for Christ. For when I am weak, then I am strong."

There will be a moment when God comes here and everything will change, and the Bible promises we will be resurrected with Christ and I have hope in that day--but for now while I am here I get to know, without a shadow of a doubt that Christ will work through me.

The same way he's working through you.

Forever with Jesus starts now. Not when you die. When you are weak, he's strong. Let that soak in. Breathe that into your lungs. Feel that in your soul.

You will get through whatever you are going through.

That's what I've learned.

And on my wedding day, with all my friends and family there and my bride in front of me, guess what? All that stuff from my past, the heartbreak, the mess, the mistakes--none of it came to mind--I didn't think about any of it. All I had was joy and hope and Kayla Rae. None of it really mattered. The future was ahead and the past was behind me.

That's what God has for you.

None of this will define you. Jesus already took it all on the cross. When he said, "it is finished" he meant it.
And if you need to remind your brain who's in control, who's boss, if you need to train your thoughts to focus on what Jesus is doing-- memorize these words that Paul says and repeat them over and over until your brain gets the picture and your thoughts quiet,

"And I am convinced that nothing can ever separate us from God's love. Neither death nor life, neither angels nor demons, neither our fears for today nor our worries about tomorrow--not even the powers of hell can separate us from God's love. No power in the sky above or in the earth below--indeed, nothing in all creation will ever be able to separate us from the love of God that is revealed in Christ Jesus our Lord.'

That's really, really good news.

STUCK AND UNSTUCK
APRIL, *JUNIOR YEAR OF HIGH SCHOOL*

We begin filming early that next morning. Driving up the gravel driveway there is a stillness in the tall evergreens, the thick blackberry bushes, the long shafts of grass silhouetted by a cold grey fog. The warm arms of sunlight had begun to creep along the edge of the hillside.

I can see Blake's mom watering hanging flowers on the deck overlooking the snowy peaked mountains. She's wearing a red wool jacket. She waves. I wave back.

Life is a series of scenes. That's just the way it is--little scenes spilling over one another. In some scenes you are stuck. In other scenes you are getting unstuck. There are a lot of things that get us stuck. What's beneath the surface of all of it is that there is a God who created you for a purpose and the good news is that the best is yet to come. The story isn't over. You are never too stuck to be unstuck.

And when you are unstuck--you are never very far from getting stuck again. That's why we need Jesus not just one time--but all the time.

Blake comes raging across the lawn on his dad's four-wheeler. Dirt cascading in an arch off the tires. Engine roaring. There's a gun rack on the side. Gravel spits in all directions. Blake has a bandana tied around his head, because I mean--*why not*? Remember that thing about how guys don't ever best friend break up?

Blake tosses me a large box; as I get out of the car, it's a brand new digital camera, a nice one.

"Alright Quentin Tarantino," he says, "let's make this freakin' movie."

I smile.

"What's this?" I ask.

"A camera."

"No, I see that."

"It's a really nice camera. Because, if we are going to make this--we have to make it right-- and we need to make it for real."

"Thanks."

"I also bought a bunch of fake blood," Blake says drumming his hands in an imaginary beat on the handlebars, "I don't know if you have a place for it, in the script, but I bought fake blood."

I reach behind me and grab the Tommy Gun that's been sitting on the back seat racking up a bill at the costume shop, "I still have this in my car," I say waving the sub-machine gun out the window, "we can make some kind of good use out of it."

Blake smiles and high-fives me.

"You're back," he says, "let's go make the most epic Spanish project the world has ever seen."

There is something deeper than happiness in the Bible.

It's joy.

Happiness is always swaying in and out of our life.

Joy is the undercurrent; it's the part of us that stands firm. But joy comes out of struggle. It's built out of pain. Joy says God is with us. Joy says the end is never really the end. Joy also comes out of forgiveness. The forgiveness that Christ gives us.

Forgiveness we have for ourselves.
And others.

Before I park in Blake's gravel driveway I stop, out in the middle of the woods I stop. The mountains, triangle snow caps poking through the clouds. My soul is still heavy. I needed to forgive her. I needed to forgive me. Forgives acknowledges wrong. It doesn't let anybody off the hook. It just says, "through Jesus I forgive you."

We can't forgive.
But through Jesus we can.

That's refreshing. That's good for your soul.

Forgiveness is the bridge to joy.

It's what I needed to feel alive. Like I was a new person.

———————

We made the movie. Took us the whole weekend. But we made it. It was heroic and beautiful and simple and forceful and didn't make any sense. The plot was less a plot and more like an indie music video where all the parts you know must fit together somehow but at the end you're really not sure how or even why. Also, it was forty-seven minutes long. We made a *forty-seven* minute Spanish project.

The class average was 7 minutes.

But, we weren't going for average.
We were going for epic.

There's one scene in particular that stands out in our movie, it's of Drew running in drab green military gear, he's holding a metal helmet against his head as it rattles around, he leaps over bushes and from behind him-- explosions (fireworks we set off in all directions, some bouncing and exploding right off of him). After which there are fistfights and jumping off cliffs, and more fireworks.

The last part of the movie took the longest to shoot. It's this slow exit where Drew's standing at the top of this water tower way out in the woods on Blake's property and he's holding this sign we make that says *the end is never the end*. It's trippy and we play a Rolling Stones song loud from a speaker and Blake, he's driving the four-wheeler and I'm on the back filming and we're circling the water tower, slow at first but then faster and faster, and I'm pointing the camera straight up at Drew--and the last shot is of this sign, we zoom in on this sign that says,

The end is never really the end.

When we turn the movie into our teacher the next week--we tell her it's almost fifty minutes long and she gives us this look that says, *why did I ever take this job.* We all have this terrible, furious look on our faces. Drew hasn't slept for 36 hours editing it all together. She looks at us and says that would take up the whole class time and we need to cut it down to at least ten minutes. We shake our heads no in unison. We protest and wave our arms. We say that we can't. We say it's art. We say it matters. We say we've worked really hard. She's not going to let us show our movie until Drew basically fake cries to her, his eyes bloodshot from not sleeping, but none of us are really sure it was fake because we are pretty sure he's delirious and really crying. Anyway, she preps the class with some bit like,

"So, this group went above and beyond and our whole class period will be watching their project."
Watching it on the small television set rolled into the class on a large black metal shelf--our

peer's stare at the screen blankly. Their expressions are boredom, confusion, or casual laughter. But we don't care. Halfway through I lean back to Blake and whisper, "we forgot to put in any Spanish." I say panicking, "We forgot to add dialog." It's totally true. There isn't a single word spoken in the whole thing. We recruited girls from school to play key parts, we added a title screen, put in our favorite rock anthems, added special effects--but didn't take the time to add any Spanish. Blake grins, leaning up towards me, "I remembered," he whispers, "but it was your movie. I didn't want to mess it up."

"We're going to fail this project," I say, "it's really going to mess up our grade."
"That's not why we made the movie," he whispers over the sound of heavy gunfire coming from the screen and fake blood--our teacher is cringing, "we would have failed probably with Spanish in it anyway," Blake says, "we made the movie so we could have something again. Something that was all of ours. Something bigger than just our lame high school drama. Something we could mess with and make all our own and love doing."

Blake was right.

There is no applause from the class when it ends. No standing ovations. It's a quiet classroom. Our teacher stares at us with this look of both absolute bewilderment and disgust. But that doesn't matter. That's not why we did it.

We did it so we could create something and try something and love something and know deep down that life can still be fun and exciting and is way too short not to blow up a bunch of fireworks in a Spanish II video. In retrospect, *yes* we should have thrown in some Spanish phrases into our project. I'm not encouraging you to fail your classes. I am encouraging you to not take things too seriously and try new things and create something epic with your life.

When I told my parents about the grade they were mad the way parents have to get when they know it's part of the job--but below the surface I sensed they were also proud, that I was stepping into a place where I wasn't hiding in my room by myself. I was embracing the life I had. I was creating again.

There's this guy that comes up to Jesus, and he asks Jesus--he says,

"What's the most important thing to pay attention to in all of the guidelines about how to live from the Bible?"

It's a good question.

What's the thing behind the thing?
What's most important?

Jesus' answer is,
"Love God and love your neighbor."
Stick to that, and you get everything else too.

I'm trying to do that.
To love God with all my heart, soul and mind.
And love people around me.

Because, I am not the center of the universe.
It isn't all about me. God is making all things
new and he doesn't waste anything.

Especially our pain.

Because, when we are weak he is strong.
Our pain is always an opportunity.

Because--the story isn't over.

The end is never really the end.